ON STUDYING POLITICAL SCIENCE

Philippa Strum

Rutgers, The State University, Newark Campus

Michael Shmidman

Borough of Manhattan Community College
The City University of New York

Goodyear Publishing Company
Pacific Palisades, California

To our respective parents

JOSEPH and IDA STRUM
RABBI ISAAC and FANNY SHMIDMAN

Library of Congress Catalog Card Number 69-17982

Current printing (last digit):
10 9 8 7 6 5 4 3 2 1

Printed in the United States of America

PREFACE

Most students beginning their first course in political science have only a vague idea of what political science is all about. They may have registered for the course because it is required, because it is being given at a convenient time, because they are mildly interested in public affairs, or because the instructor has the reputation of being very good or of giving high marks. Very few students understand the nature and purpose of the social sciences in general and political science in particular. Unfortunately, most instructors, having to convey more information about American government or Western political ideas than they can possibly cover in one semester, are forced to plunge directly into the subject matter and cannot take time to explain the characteristics of the discipline involved. We hope that this volume will help to fill the gap by introducing the student to the whats and whys of political science: the material studied by the political scientist, the objectives he pursues, the techniques and methodologies he utilizes, the validity of his conclusions, etc. Since this work is designed to be an elementary introduction, a great many things have been left out and a great many others have been glossed over. The authors nevertheless believe that this book will serve a useful function in beginning courses by enabling the student to become familiar with political science and by freeing the instructor for the pursuit of substantive matters.

It is expected that *On Studying Political Science* will be read by the student at the inception of the course, and because high school civics courses will undoubtedly have given him some degree of familiarity with American institutions, we have drawn our examples from the American political system.

Our thanks go to the many students who have taught us much of what we know, and to Professor Walter Weiker, who has generously contributed his wise advice and comments. Responsibility for the specific form and content of all the material in the book, of course, is ours alone.

P.S.
M.S.

CONTENTS

V

INTRODUCTION:
TO THE STUDENT

Now that you have registered for this introductory course in political science—or, perhaps, now that you have been registered in it by an electronic device—you may well ask yourself, "Political science—what's it all about? Will this course be a continuation of my high school civics and American history courses, with the only differences being that now I will have to memorize even more facts and dates and that I may have to write a term paper? And what does 'political science' mean, anyway?"

The purpose of this book is to show you that political science, as one of the social sciences, is not merely

1

a conglomeration of facts and dates, but is devoted to the study of man: his behavior, his interaction with his fellow human beings, and the institutions that he helps to create. Political science attempts to discover why it is that man establishes various institutions and how and why they function. It asks why man has chosen to give up some of his liberty to a group of people who constitute "authority" and who can force him to perform—or not perform—in certain ways. It tries to find out which individuals and groups have power, how they got it, and how they use it. In general, it approaches government and laws and regulations as man-made institutions that can be analyzed and understood and altered.

The authors hope that this book will help you to realize that government is but one of the institutions that man, a social animal, establishes to make his life more meaningful and to solve problems that he alone cannot handle. All the facts gathered by political scientists are of little value unless it is clearly understood that everything governments do is the result of societal values and of decisions societies have made about the functions that governments should fulfill. People, having needs and values, establish institutions to answer the needs in ways dictated by the values. Should the governmental system they create prove incapable of satisfying their needs, whatever they may be—and political science is concerned with the nature of needs and why it is that people in different societies express similar and different needs—that government will not long be governing.

Political science, then, is not solely the study of politics per se. Its major concern is human behavior. It is not so much the study of particular laws as it is the study of why it is that people make laws, how they go about making them, and what institutions they create and utilize in the process. To reiterate: Political science is devoted less to the "what" of government than it is to the "why" and "how." This, then, is the lesson of the following chapters.

Chapter *1*

THE NATURE OF POLITICAL SCIENCE

After Adam and Eve had been created, it became only a matter of time until political science developed.

Adam and Eve's offspring multiplied and their "begats" begot until the world was so well populated that a number of societies came into existence. With so many people on this planet, ground rules had to be established if its inhabitants were not to get in each other's way. One of the rules had to be that men could not wander around wantonly murdering each other; otherwise, no man could feel safe enough to devote himself to the everyday matters of living. Similarly, restrictions had to be placed on the

3

taking of a man's food or shelter or wife, or no man could feel secure in his possessions. One would think that everybody would abide by these home truths, but even in post-Eden, not everybody did (as witness a gentleman named Cain). People who murdered or stole had to be punished so that others would be dissuaded from following their example. At first, punishment was an individual affair: If X killed Y, members of Y's family would go after X. Unfortunately, this would disturb the members of X's family, and they would usually go running after some member of Y's family. People began to realize that this was rather self-defeating, because everyone was ultimately related to either X's family or Y's family or both, and if the process was kept up long enough no one would be left. It was also discovered that if B accused C of theft, and C denied it, someone had to be around to settle the quarrel. Moreover, people involved in the everyday tasks of obtaining food and clothing and shelter and raising children and getting along with one another found that they had no time to settle other people's quarrels. Similarly, they could not drop everything to go chasing after a thief or to deal with emissaries from other societies. What they needed was some organization or functionary whom everyone could trust and who could be counted on to inflict just punishment, settle disputes, and generally handle matters that no one else had time for. And so, government was born.

The big problem then became who was to constitute the government, what functions it would perform, who would decide who was to constitute the government, and who would decide what functions it was to perform. The attempt to answer these questions led to the rise of politicians, and, inevitably, to the development of political science.

If this seems to be a perfunctory and somewhat facetious oversimplification, it nevertheless presents the outlines of the story. Governments came into existence because men found that they needed an institution that would do for them things they could not do for themselves. Political science, which is the study of governments and of the political actors and events that surround them, evolved as a method for evaluating and choosing the wisest possible system. The essence of politics is the struggle of human beings to obtain the power to answer the questions mentioned above, and the essence of political science is the investigation and analysis of human behavior within the area commonly labeled political.

Many of the decisions about the nature of government and the allocation of power are embodied in laws. Laws represent agreements as to how people and institutions shall behave, and in this they are similar to many other kinds of societal agreements. In all societies, members reach agreement on rules intended to govern or influence societal behavior. Although all such rules are voluntarily agreed to, not all of them carry the sanction of law and the potential of enforcement by law officers. It is generally agreed within American society, for example, that women shall wear skirts and men shall wear trousers; that men shall work at money-producing jobs in order to support themselves and their families; that one of the signs of "respectability" is membership in a church. As both recent fashions and the "hippies" have shown, however, it is possible for Americans to ignore the agreement about who shall wear trousers; beggars prove that men can obtain a livelihood without working; and the despair of many churches today is a general lack of interest in religion and church membership. All of these agreements, then, can be safely ignored or violated by individuals or groups. They are voluntary agreements, backed up by no more than the force of society's approval or disapproval. This does not mean that they are not binding upon most members of the society. The individual who arrives at a church wedding dressed in Bermuda shorts may find himself isolated from at least some segments of society. In psychological or economic terms, penalties for noncompliance with the rules may be severe. Nevertheless, the stouthearted can choose to flout them.

Laws are somewhat different. No one can disobey them with impunity. A thief, an arsonist, or a murderer will quickly discover that there is no permissible deviance from the rules against interference with life or property. Why should this be the case? Why may a man ignore the church-membership agreement or the church dress codes, but not the property-ownership agreement?

The answer is to be found in the understanding that all societal agreements represent a consensus of values, but that there is a hierarchy of values in every society. We place a value on proper dress, on employment, on church membership, on the sanctity of property, and on the sanctity of life. Some of our values, however, are considered to be more important than others. Some of them, indeed, are considered to be so important that it is decided that no one shall be allowed to violate them, and that anyone who ignores them shall suffer severe consequences. We place such a high value on life and property that we are willing to back up those values with the coercive force of the government: Violators will be forcibly punished. This, then, is the difference between laws and what we might call customs or mores or social norms: The values embodied in laws are so basic to the society which holds them that they must be obeyed by all, and to make certain that they are obeyed, their enforcement is entrusted to the only organization in society that is given the right to use force. In short: The more important the value, the more stringent the sanction.

This should not be taken to mean that government exists only to create and enforce laws against criminals. We have laws establishing a Social Security system that provides for older people, laws providing for government funding of dormitory construction and theatrical groups, laws designed to further space exploration. Enforcement of these laws implies tasks of administration rather than of chasing criminals. The laws themselves reflect the value our society places on the financial security of the old, on college education, and on cultural enterprises and scientific investigation. They also reflect the general agreement that these objectives cannot be accomplished by individuals or small groups, but must be approached through the broad collective action that we call government.

Since laws are an expression of a society's values, social change —an alteration in the environment that creates values—usually precedes legal change. When Congress rebuffed President Kennedy on his proposed Medicare legislation, Kennedy predicted that a bill encompassing his objective would nevertheless be passed within a relatively few years. He was able to make the prediction because he was aware that the society itself was changing: that such phenomena as the civil rights movement and the country's soaring affluence were leading to a recognition that no one need do or ought to do without essential services; that there was a growing proportion of citizens over 65, due in part, paradoxically enough, to improved medical care throughout life; that illness usually accompanies longevity; that the combination of constant and spiraling inflation and long-term illness could wipe out a lifetime's savings and make pension income valueless; that children might not be able to bear the financial burden of elderly parents' extended illnesses, especially as medical and hospital costs increased; that it was becoming common knowledge that economic forces can victimize the hardest working and most virtuous citizen. He understood further that as the social changes led to alterations in values—that is, increased emphasis on the desirability of medical care for the aged, no matter what their financial situation, along with a willingness to be taxed in order to provide funds for such care— the new values would find expression in laws directing the government's administrative apparatus to make use of its resources for the alleviation of the newly perceived social problem.

Almost twenty years before the passage of a Medicare bill, President Truman had advocated similar legislation. The length of time between original proposal and ultimate enactment is an indication of the slowness with which the legal system is wont to change. There are two reasons for this. The first is that in a country as large and diversified as the United States, many different values can be found at any given moment, and it necessarily requires a good deal of time before they can be reconciled or before one value can achieve sufficient agreement to be codified into law. Second, society is frequently unsure of its values. Most citizens are not given to reflection about their beliefs and views, which means that when they are faced with a social problem, they may not know exactly how they feel about it. Even if they are given to reflection, however, the permutations of any social problem are usually so great and so confusing that it may take time for most people to decide what their reactions to it should be. Occasionally, an event of shocking proportions may be required to make them aware of their own values. Thus, the passage of the 1964 Civil Rights Act can be attributed in part to the television pictures of civil rights marchers being attacked by police dogs and by sheriffs wielding cattle prods and to the assassination of President Kennedy, just as the enactment of the 1968 Open Housing bill was largely the result of the assassination of the Rev. Dr. Martin Luther King. Both bills, tied up in public controversy and congressional maneuvering, had been the victims of the American people's inability to decide whether their values demanded the bills' passage or defeat; both were passed when events occurred to catalyze Americans into recognition of and general agreement about their feelings. Most laws, however, are enacted after a lengthy but less spectacular period of assessment and reassessment of values.

Several ways in which laws can be used have been suggested by the examples above. Law is a social instrument; that is, it is one of the methods by which a society implements programs and changes it judges to be desirable. It is far from the only social instrument available, however. Society as a whole may place a positive value on medical research but may choose to have the bulk of such research carried out by private individuals, institutions, foundations, health centers, etc., rather than involve the government in that sphere. As a rule, law is used as a social instrument only when there is widespread agreement that a societal need exists and that no agency other than the government can fill it as fully or efficiently as society wishes.

Law is one element in a society's procedural consensus, which is to say that it depicts some of the important ground rules that the society has agreed upon for the formulation and implementation of political change. American law decrees that citizens who want to institute political change shall be free to discuss their beliefs in public or to explain them in articles and books, but that they cannot blow up Congress in order to dramatize their point of view without suffering the consequences of criminal proceedings—and this in turn implies that the attractiveness of their cause will be diminished in the public mind. If they manage to convince the society that a particular change is desirable and that it should be embodied in a law, basic American law also describes the methodology for its enactment: If it is to be a federal law, for example, it must be passed by both houses of Congress, signed by the President, etc. Not all of a society's ground rules are translated into law, although, in the United States and other Western countries, the most important ones usually are.

Law can also be seen as an expression of morality. It puts into words and into programs of action the beliefs shared by much of a society as to what is good and just and desirable. The existence of the Medicare program in effect constitutes an announcement that it is good for all elderly people to receive proper medical care; that it is good for the society as a whole, utilizing the government as its instrument, to ensure the availability of that care; that it is good to ignore a person's earlier earning capacity or thrift or industry and consider only his medical needs in deciding what aid he should be given. The morality found in a law may stem from religious tenets ("Thou shalt not kill"), from basic constitutional principles, from the lessons of particular events, etc., but no matter what its source, every law necessarily carries with it the implication that something is good and that its opposite is not. Laws thus reflect many of the ideals of a society.

In addition, law is an expression and protector of the status quo. It is a statement of the distribution of social, economic, and political power that exists in a society at a given moment. It is a means of protecting the power distribution. A law giving the right to vote only to citizens over twenty-one years of age retains political power for those defined as "adults" and effectively disenfranchises everyone who does not yet fall into that category. It renders those under twenty-one relatively powerless politically and places the power to alter the situation solely in the hands of those over twenty-one. In effect, it protects the political power of those who already have it. Similarly, laws that extend minimum wage coverage only to certain categories of workers and exclude others both ensure the relative economic powerlessness of citizens in the excluded categories and secure the economic power of those who employ them. Law in its role as an expression of the status quo is thus the protector of the particular social, economic, and political interests that benefit from the existence of the status quo. Changes in the law merely help to create, express, and protect a new status quo.

Laws are created and administered by the government and by all the individuals and groups that cause the government to take specific actions. Government is established by society to articulate and enforce laws, which in turn reflect some of society's most cherished values and the decision of its members to organize an institution that will do for them what they cannot do for themselves, individually or as smaller groups. It differs from other voluntary associations within the society in its size, its location, and the extent of its authority. Unlike other groups, which rarely embrace more than a large minority of citizens, the government's constituency includes all citizens (and, it might be added, all other voluntary associations as well). It can be located in space—border disputes or uncertainties notwithstanding, all governments exercise authority over specific territorial areas. The authority of government is both broad and final. Even the most laissez-faire of governments will find itself involved in many areas of human endeavor, and, as we have seen, it alone has the right to regulate the use of force within its borders.

Other voluntary organizations are similar to governments in that they too are established to represent certain interests and achieve certain results that individuals acting singly cannot hope to obtain. The interests they represent are usually narrower and less universal than those encompassed by a government. Nongovernmental organizations may be able to satisfy their comparatively limited desires without having recourse to the official governmental mechanism or the use of coercion. Nevertheless, although the appeal to the governmental power is but one facet of their attempt to achieve their aims, they—and individuals—will sometimes find themselves calling upon the government to take action.

Politics is the method by which the decisions as to how and when the government will and will not act are made. It can be described as a struggle for the power to control the making of those decisions. It has also been called the "art of the possible," or the process by which the conflicting demands of various individuals and groups are satisfied through compromise. Different demands for action or inaction on the part of government are made by different segments of the population. The formulation and presentation of demands is one aspect of politics. Political actors will then jockey either for the power to make the government's decisions or for influence over those who will make the decisions. Finally, through negotiations and compromise among interested parties, the decisions will be made and carried out. All of these steps are part of the political process.

The political desires shared by the members of a society impel them to create a government and a political system. The desires that they do not share will lead to struggle within the society and within the political system which is a part of it. In this sense, the political system exists both as a codification of the means agreed upon for the attainment of shared political desires and as a formal methodology for the resolution of conflicting desires. "Political" here connotes "power," so that political desires can be differentiated from others by the insistence of individuals and groups that the fulfillment of them must be given binding force throughout the society.

Since the demands made on government by members of society are an expression of the members' values and an indication of what they believe *should* be done, political science is not only the study of government and of the behavior of people who try to influence the government, but the study of societal values as well. Without knowledge of a society's values and aspirations, no political scientist can hope to understand the nature and workings of its governmental system.

In broad terms, then, political science is the study of the following: the reasons and values behind the formulation of particular demands for binding decisions made by the society and segments thereof; the way in which the demands are formulated and communicated; the structures, institutions, and techniques established by the society to evaluate and deal with demands; the specific functions performed by the various structures individually and by the combination of structures as a whole; the political role performed by nonpolitical institutions; the dynamic by which the structures arrive at a response to the demands and the method by which competing demands are resolved; the way in which governmental responses to demands are communicated and applied; the way governmental responses in turn both create new demands and alter the existing structures; the variety of political roles available to would-be political actors; and the methodologies and criteria utilized by the society in deciding whether particular uses of power are legitimate. All of these phenomena are aspects of politics, and all are within the area studied by the political scientist.

Political science and the social sciences

Political science is one of the disciplines which take as their subject the behavior of man in society and are therefore called social sciences. They include, besides political science, psychology, sociology, anthropology, economics, and perhaps history. In order to understand just what political science is, one must consider its relationship with the other social sciences and the ways in which it parallels and differs from them.

Man is the greatest of all problem solvers. Much of his behavior stems from his need to develop sets of answers to the basic problems of living. On the most primitive level, he must learn how to obtain food, clothing, and shelter in order to survive. He must learn how to go about living with others and how to create a pattern of child rearing so that human life and society as he knows it will be perpetuated. He must learn to cope with all the problems of nature so as to perpetuate and perhaps improve human existence. Finally, he must deal with the problem of human power and the decision as to who within his society shall have control over whom; who shall lead and who shall follow.

A society is any group of people who live and interact with each other. The answers they develop to the basic problems of life become their culture, or the sum total of ways of living which they follow and will transmit to successive generations. They will decide that certain substances may be eaten and that others may not; that shelters should be built of certain materials and in certain shapes; that certain parts of the body should be covered in certain ways; that it is desirable for people in a certain blood relationship with one another to mate and have children, but taboo for others to do so; that certain members of the group shall have the right to determine the actions of others, etc. Every society works out such collective commands and customs. We in the United States, for example, have decided that beef and potatoes and breakfast cereals are acceptable foods but that snakes and grasshoppers are not; that in everyday life women may bare their legs although men cannot, but that all may do so in certain places such as beaches; that children should be raised by their parents rather than by the society as a whole or by extended groups of relatives; that the leaders of our society should be elected by all adult citizens, no matter how poor or ignorant some of them may be, rather than be chosen only by those with large incomes or those with college degrees. These answers constitute our culture. Most of them were given to us by our parents and most of them will be passed on by us to our children.

In accepting and organizing particular answers to the problems of life, we come to put a positive value on them. We believe that our solutions are good, we know that they have worked in the past, and we expect all future solutions to new problems to incorporate the proven values we already possess. Thus, since early frontier Americans solved the problem of how a man was to go about supporting his family by decreeing that he would be free to exercise his initiative and begin whatever farm or store or other business that he liked—and, it should be understood, this solution was necessitated by conditions of life on the frontier, where land and economic opportunity were abundant, neighbors were far removed from each other, and no one could be expected to solve a man's economic problems but that man himself—we today put a positive value on economic liberty and tend initially to be skeptical of governmental programs that seem to infringe upon it. The value persists and will undoubtedly continue to do so for some time, even though we now live in a crowded urban society that filled out its land frontiers long ago.

Culture, then, consists of a society's answers to the problems of living and the values that emerge from those answers. The political process is an integral part of culture. Government is an answer to the particular problem of how a society will choose the leaders who will do for its citizens the things they cannot do for themselves and how the leaders will behave. There are many possible kinds of government. A society will be limited in its selection of the kind of government it wants by its culture and the values incorporated in it. When the American Revolution was ended and the people had to choose a form of government, for example, they relied on their beliefs that government should be close to the people and that no government should have a great deal of power, and they chose to spread out primary political power among the state governments. Given the existing post-revolutionary society and its values, as well as its experiences under English rule, suggestions that the government be a strong centralized body or that the people elect to be ruled by an aristocracy simply could not be accepted.

To say that the political process is an integral part of the culture is to say that the political process cannot be fully understood without some knowledge of the culture of which it is a part. Government, after all, is a man-made contrivance. Its existence represents a decision of men that it is necessary to construct an institution which will satisfy otherwise unfulfillable individual and societal needs. This means that no political scientist can possibly hope to discuss legislation or other governmental acts unless he knows what the needs of the society are, what its values are, why it chose Political System A instead of Political System B or C, and why it once believed it could get along without a particular piece of legislation but now feels that it is necessary. An example of this can be found in the problem of parity payments to American farmers.

Federal law permits the government to pay farmers not to grow food. The parity law is based on the theory that if farmers grow all that they can, their products will flood the market, prices will fall, and they will no longer receive adequate compensation for their work. It is argued that if they simply stop growing food on some of their land, their profit on the remainder will still not be enough to provide them with a livelihood. The solution adopted by the government has been to pay them not to grow food on a portion of their land, and thus to subsidize them. Quite obviously, since parity payments are embodied in a law, and laws are among the major elements of a political system, parity payments fall within the intellectual area studied by the political scientist. And yet, if one examines the problem of the farmer and parity payments, one discovers that the origin of the farmer's plight has very little to do with political science. Its genesis can be explained in the language of economics, and has to do with what might be called either overproduction or underconsumption: Because of modern technology and modern farm methods, farmers today produce more goods than the American consumer is willing to buy. The law of supply and demand inexorably drives down the price of farm goods. Since the law of supply and demand is a law of economics and not one created by the government, it might appear that the farm problem should be solved by the economist rather than the political scientist. But, as we shall see, economists can no more claim a monopoly over this problem than can political scientists.

The sociologist and the social psychologist can also shed light on the causes of the farm problem. One of the realities of American life is that we have become far more carnivorous than herbivorous. We are no longer a nation of bread-eaters. Modern American society lives in terror of obesity. We are the Pepsi generation, constantly on the go and refusing to carry as much as an extra ounce of weight— or so we would like to believe. We chatter knowingly about the dangers of cholesterol and the scientific findings of the relationship of fat to cardiac diseases. We have become meat-eaters rather than wheat-eaters, and artificial-food consumers above all. The chances are good that you and your classmates did not have hot cereal for breakfast this morning. By not doing so, you have certainly contributed to the plight of the farmer. Cereal producers buy less of his corn and wheat because many Americans content themselves with a fast cup of artificially sweetened instant coffee in the morning.

There is yet another aspect to the parity problem. Most Americans, rural or urban, put a positive value on measures to preserve and support a farm population that is perhaps larger than is merited by purely economic considerations. We in the United States enjoy what has been called the "agrarian mystique," namely the belief that farmers and those close to the land are somehow purer, less affected, and more desirable as people than are other human beings. We cannot discuss here all the reasons for the existence of this myth. It is sufficient to note that it dates back to Colonial times and to such respected men as Thomas Jefferson, who considered tillers of the soil to be God's chosen people. What is important for our purposes is the realization that when Americans consider the farm problem, their reaction is not entirely objective but is colored by an already-made value judgment. And values lie within the realms of the psychologist and the sociologist.

Neither the American psychology nor the laws of economics appear to fall into the domain of the political scientist, and yet the parity payment law is a governmental enactment and so it is, after all, fit for his consideration. The farmer, in his plight, turned neither to economists nor sociologists for aid. He turned to the government. Although economics and sociology helped to explain the genesis of the problem, neither discipline offered a solution satisfactory to the farmer. It is only government, with its great resources and ability to determine the allocation of these resources, that can utilize man-made law to undo the side effects of technological advances and altered eating habits. Government can ameliorate the impact of social and technical forces which, if ignored, might victimize certain segments of the population.

The farmers therefore sought aid from the government. The farm lobby, congressmen from affected rural areas, small-town merchants whose livelihood depends on the affluence of local farmers, consumers who oppose higher prices for farm goods, congressmen from urban areas—all became involved in expressing their views of the situation and in presenting demands for or against governmental action. At this point, the farm problem became proper subject matter for the political scientist, for the maneuvering of various groups in their attempts to influence the course followed by the government are his concern. Economists and sociologists can explain why the farm problem exists; it is up to political scientists to show what political forces persuaded the government to enact parity laws and why opposing forces were unsuccessful. Even in their own domain, however, the political scientists were aided by the psychologists' analysis of the importance of the agrarian mystique to the average American and the way in which that psychological factor could become an element in the political process.

Here we have an illustration of the relationship of the social sciences to one another. They are complementary parts of a whole, but it is a whole too broad to be encompassed within one discipline. The subject of the social studies is all of mankind: its behavior, its accomplishments, its desires, its values. Clearly, this enormous area cannot be studied all at one time. The compartmentalization of the social sciences is an organizational device designed to facilitate study and understanding. Within certain limits, the compartments make sense. There is no need for someone interested in the reasons for the parity law to study the sociology of an industrial plant. On the other hand, there is every reason for him to study the sociology of the Pepsi generation.

It should be remembered, then, that the boundary lines among the social sciences are arbitrary and elastic. The political scientist must be aware of the other social sciences and will frequently depend upon them to illuminate his own studies.

There are two other connections between political science and its fellow social sciences. One lies in the political role played by groups and institutions not usually thought of as being political. The other involves the necessity to invite the aid of other social sciences in the solutions of problems that confront the government.

Corporations, unions, interest groups such as the American Medical Association and the National Education Association, and churches all involve themselves in the political process at various times. This will be discussed more fully below (see, Who Acts Politically, p. 28). For the moment, it is sufficient to point out that when they do act politically, these groups are of interest to the political scientist, and yet it should be obvious that he cannot fully analyze their demands and techniques without calling upon information gathered by other social sciences. He cannot understand the government's reactions to corporation demands unless he has an idea of the economic impact of a few large corporations upon the entire nation. He cannot comprehend the program of the American Medical Association without the sociologist's insights into the kind of leadership and group dynamics that such an organization is likely to have. Thus, because groups that are political only secondarily nonetheless participate in political life, the political scientist finds himself dependent upon his brother social scientists—as they, in turn, find themselves dependent upon him.

Any governmental attempt to alleviate societal ills is fit subject matter for the political scientist. The government, however, frequently turns to other social scientists in its search for solutions. Hence, the political scientist must have some familiarity with other disciplines in order to understand the rationale behind many government acts.

An example can be found in the government's efforts to deal with race relations in this country. The first key governmental action in the recent history of race relations was the 1954 Supreme Court decision declaring segregated schools to be in violation of the Constitution. The Court argued that the old standard, "separate but equal," had no validity, since the compulsory separation of black and white students carried with it such psychological and sociological discrimination that black schools could not possibly be considered "equal." In support of its argument, the Court cited a variety of psychological and sociological texts. No true understanding of the Court's decision can be achieved without some knowledge of the kind of evidence which it found in the texts and which, it claimed, formed the very foundation of its decision. Here, the decision of a governmental agency was based on information gathered by other social sciences.

The first major piece of civil rights legislation in this century was the 1964 Civil Rights Act. Although it specifically mentioned such political rights as voting, much of the Act entailed the recognition that such problems as segregated eating places, unequal employment opportunities, segregated schools, etc., while not directly involving political rights, were inextricably related to the political process and the distribution of power made possible by that process. Again, neither the genesis nor the wisdom of the Act can be analyzed unless one has some familiarity with the kinds of nonpolitical problems it sought to solve.

Finally, the 1968 report of the President's National Advisory Commission on Civil Disorders indicated the impossibility of confining political action to traditionally political areas. According to the Commission, race relations in the United States cannot be stabilized until white people become conscious of and begin to eliminate their prejudices against black people, and black people are given extensive aid in such areas as finding decent jobs and housing. The Commission thus advocated action by governmental agencies not only in the areas of economics and sociology but in the psychological field as well. In order to participate meaningfully in such action, political scientists must work hand in hand with economists, sociologists, and psychologists. If they are to be socially and academically effective, they must journey beyond the artificial confines of their discipline and develop a familiarity with other approaches to the problems of man.

To summarize: The boundary lines among the various social sciences are arbitrary attempts to divide a huge field of study into manageable segments. It would be self-defeating for political scientists —or any other social scientists, for that matter—to forget that the boundaries exist not because they possess any inherent validity but simply as an organizational tool. The problems of human life are expressed in many ways and on many levels, some of them "political" and some of them not. Anyone who wishes to understand and discuss these problems must be prepared to approach them from a multiplicity of angles.

The uniqueness of political science

Political science is distinguished from its fellow social sciences by its concern with the legal government of a nation or other political subdivision and the attempts made by various individuals and groups to influence the actions of the government. It studies the governing of men and the governmental institutions established in order to solve public problems—that is, those problems which are perceived by the citizenry as a whole and/or their representatives as requiring the power and resources of the government for solution—and to enhance the quality of life. The social sciences in general are concerned with human behavior; political science is distinctive for its interest in the political behavior of individuals and the political institutions they establish. It deals with the questions of what impels men to create institutions that will necessarily and inevitably limit the liberty of the individuals who created them, even while they may enhance the general liberty and freedom; what societal needs and values lead to the creation of different political institutions in different societies; on what basis political power is allocated; what kinds of rules and regulations are considered necessary for the perpetuation and advancement of particular societies; what political beliefs men hold, and why; how both citizens and officials exercise their power; the methods by which men seek to achieve political power; the uses to which they put it; the influence of political activities on spheres not usually considered to be political, and vice versa; the limitations various societies place on political power; etc.

It should be remembered that, along with the other social sciences, political science involves more than analysis and description. It is not merely an observer of the political scene, but an active participant as well. Political scientists concern themselves with the problems facing their societies and with the methods by which governmental institutions can hope to ameliorate them. Political science would be a sterile and remote endeavor if its lessons could not be translated into positive action. Thus, its practitioners are to be found at all levels of government, usually in advisory positions, as well as in public movements and organizations of various kinds.

This is not meant to imply that it is only political scientists who utilize their professional skills in the service of the government and the public, or that all political scientists are actively engaged in public life. Because of its involvement in a broad spectrum of human affairs, the government must call upon the advisory talents of individuals from a great many walks of life: economists, sociologists, lawyers, doctors, and engineers, among others. Political scientists, however, are particularly well qualified to deal with the ways in which governmental activity is and can be directed toward the fulfillment of societal needs. They can go beyond showing the government what approach to problems it might take. Uniquely, they can suggest the best ways for the government to formulate its policies so that, as the policies are filtered down through the political apparatus, they will actually and efficiently achieve the desired results. Political scientists, in other words, can illuminate the administrative process for the policy maker.

The understanding of the political system—the hallmark of the political scientist—stems in large measure from research into that system. Thus, at any given moment, more political scientists will be spending more of their time thinking, studying, investigating, and publishing the results of their intellectual endeavors than will be partly or exclusively engaged in public activities. Nevertheless, it should be emphasized that political science would be no more than an ivory tower pastime were its lessons merely passed on from one political scientist to another.

The relationship between the theoretical and the practical is illustrated by the number of political scientists whose entrance into the political arena has reflected both their interest in the political process and their desire to bring their expertise to the service of government. Perhaps the most illustrious of these former academicians was Woodrow Wilson; more recent examples are Hubert Humphrey and George McGovern. Other political scientists have entered government life in less publicized roles.

Conversely, practicing politicians have much of value to tell the political scientists. Political scholars frequently invite elected and appointed officials and others active in the political world to speak to them about their experiences with the intricacies of politics. Former high officials are particularly in demand: No matter what his partisan views might be, almost any political scientist would gladly accept an invitation to attend Lyndon Johnson's lectures on policy making and the nature of government.

Thus, theoretical inquiry can be of great importance to the practitioners of the political art, and political actors can aid in the formulation and evaluation of theories. Political science draws on both theory and experience. It can be called a "social" science not only because it investigates social phenomena but also because it utilizes its findings to serve society's attempts to discover means by which it can alleviate the problems and enhance the lives of its members.

Political science and "science"

In a good many colleges, what we have been referring to as the study of political science is called the study of government. It is quite understandable that courses about different types of governments and governmental institutions are sometimes simply called "government courses." It may seem strange to some students, however, that the study of government and of political institutions is sometimes called "political science." Hence, the question arises: Can the study of political actors and institutions be labeled a science?

To a great degree, the answer depends upon one's definition of "science" and "scientific method." If by "science" one means absolute predictability of events—the knowledge that a given cause will invariably produce a certain result—then one necessarily should exclude the study of politics from the realm of the scientific. The study of political actors and political institutions is the study of human beings and human institutions, and the only constant in the human world is change and the existence of forces of change. Human nature and action are often unpredictable. Unlike the planets or a combination of chemicals or a weed, man has the ability to choose his course of action, and thus he may frequently confound the "scientists."

An example can be found in studies of voting behavior. Analysts have discovered that American Catholics, taken as a whole, tend to vote Democratic. This is especially true of Catholics in the lower socioeconomic levels. Urban dwellers, members of labor unions, those whose parents voted Democratic—all tend to vote Democratic. If Mr. A is a lower-middle class urban Catholic laborer whose parents are faithful Democrats, then, it seems fairly certain that his vote will be found in the Democratic column. And yet, because he resents a particular Democratic candidate's accent, or because he had a stomach-ache on the day he heard the candidate speak and came away angry with the world in general and the party in power in particular, or because he wants to show his independence and refuses to vote the way family and friends do, or simply because he made a mistake in the voting booth and pulled the wrong lever, Mr. A may have helped to elect a Republican senator. Planets don't have whims or stomach-aches or accidents; human beings do.

Given this human clay as the basic material of his study, then, how can the political analyst claim to be a scientist? If he had tried to predict the way Mr. A would vote, he would have been wrong. His analysis appears to have fallen short of the classic scientific requirement of absolute predictability.

There is, however, an alternative definition of science and scientific method. Science can be defined as the organization of generally accepted principles; what is meant by scientific method may best be explained as follows:

1. The researcher is utilizing scientific method if he gathers empirical evidence—evidence of past events that can be verified—and employs it to illuminate his research.

2. The researcher is employing scientific method when he reports his procedures and findings in such a manner that other researchers using the same procedures and evidence will arrive at the same conclusions.

3. The researcher is following scientific method when he accords the highest position to empirical evidence, ignoring his own values and presuppositions as far as is humanly possible.

Given these criteria, can the study of politics be called scientific? Let us return to the example of voting behavior.

Is it possible to accumulate empirical evidence in this area? Quite obviously, statistics can be gathered from urban areas, from neighborhoods in which the average income is below a certain level, from areas in which the majority of the population is Catholic, etc. If information from these places indicates a repeated overwhelming vote for Democratic candidates, it can rightly be claimed that the information has illuminated research into the problem of what factors lead to citizens' voting for the donkey rather than the elephant. It should be relatively easy to present the statistics clearly enough to enable any researcher to draw conclusions from them; and, if the original analyst has done his work properly, the conclusions of later analysts can be expected to coincide with his own.

What the analyst will have done is to collect information, distinguish factor upon factor, and organize his analysis of the information into general principles. He may have begun with the theory that Catholics tend to vote Democratic. If he found evidence to support the theory, he must then have asked himself a number of questions. Why do Catholics tend to vote Democratic? It is not a result of genetics, nor is it a matter of church dogma. This can be proven by the tendency of Catholics in the upper economic strata to vote Democratic less frequently than those in the lower economic strata. Clearly, religion is not the sole factor in determining voting behavior; economics also plays a role. Which, then, is the more important factor? Is it religion or economics, or perhaps a combination of the two? Are there additional factors—place of residence, type of employment, educational level—which affect voting behavior?

Having answered these questions, the political analyst can legitimately claim to have completed a scientific study. He has utilized empirical evidence to establish general principles which he can expect to be confirmed *more frequently than not*. He has undertaken a study designed to determine what series of events or factors may lead to particular human behavior. He has not fashioned a law along the lines of H_2O = water. H_2O will equal water no matter when or where the elements are combined, but a voter complete with all the characteristics of a potential Democrat may nevertheless choose to vote for a Republican. The political scientist has simply presented us with a measure of predictability where, before, there was none.

The political scientist must guard against his own potentially unscientific behavior as well as against that of those he studies. Any scientist, physical or social, may fall prey to his desire to make a particular point no matter what the evidence may say. All scientists must govern their intellectual behavior rigorously by following the evidence wherever it leads and by refusing to allow their conclusions to precede their proof. The social scientist, however, has an additional problem in adhering to the third criterion of scientific method.

A geologist trying to ascertain the age of a rock need not care whether the rock turns out to be 2,000,000 years old or 2,500,000 (unless, of course, he has previously committed himself to one of those figures). He is interested only in determining its age, whatever it may be. His life style, in all probability, will not be altered by his conclusion. He will not join in popular campaigns to make rocks older. His behavior cannot change the age of the rock; that is an unalterable "given." The political scientist, on the other hand, may very well have a stake in the material he is examining. On the simplest level, a political scientist writing about the political decisions made by a recent President will have voted for or against that President and will want his criticism or praise of the President's actions to bear out the wisdom of his own vote. Or he may be studying the behavior of a political group which he has been brought up to believe is undesirable. Should the President for whom he voted turn out to have acted unwisely, or should the group he disdains prove to have a number of good ideas, he will be forced to reexamine his own preconceptions and prejudices. All human beings have values and biases of which they are unaware; delving into them and possibly changing them can be a painful business, for it requires the admission that the ideas were incorrect and that the human beings involved are fallible and may still be making errors of judgment in other matters. Most of the ideas important to people concern other people, rather than inert entities or laws of motion or combustion. It is therefore the scientist engaged in the study of people who is most likely to find his preconceptions getting in his way. The political scientist is more often than not an actor in the very drama he has chosen to observe and describe.

In spite of his involvement in the dramas he will describe, no honest political scientist deliberately sets out to misconstrue evidence, nor does he willingly allow his biases to color his conclusions. The problem is precisely that such preconceptions are largely unconscious, so that the political scientist must constantly stop and ask himself whether he has unintentionally allowed personal feelings to interfere with his scientific objectivity. This is a difficulty of which the student must also be aware, for the very questions to which his readings are devoted may be couched in such a subjective manner that they necessarily distort the evidence and result in biased conclusions. The political scientist thus battles continually against the attributes that make him human.

Assuming that the battle can be won and that the researcher has carefully assembled empirical data and drawn conclusions that can be verified by his colleagues, it does not seem excessive to claim that a scientific study has taken place. General rules have been posited and have been found to be correct more often than not. Human behavior has been explained and predicted with a certain degree of accuracy. It may be suggested, then, that while the practice of politics is an art, the study of that art and of the political actor can indeed be called scientific.

The fact-value distinction

One of the basic distinctions that must be made by both political scientists and students is that between facts and values. Factual statements are those that can be proven or disproven empirically. The statements that the House of Representatives consists of 435 members and that the Senate has a number of standing committees are factual. They indicate no prejudice or partiality on the part of their author; they can be verified empirically. To say that the House of Representatives is behind the times, however, or that the Senate functions inefficiently, is to indulge in a value judgment reflecting the personal feelings of its author. Neither statement can be proven empirically, if only because the definition of "behind the times" or "functions inefficiently" is debatable. This does not mean that value judgments have no validity. They function as hypotheses; as ideas deserving further investigation. We all make value judgments constantly and legitimately; we must decide for ourselves what is good and what is bad, what is right and what is wrong. The key words are "for ourselves": The danger of others' value judgments is that we may misread them for factual statements and accept them without question.

Value judgments which are seemingly borne out by statistics are perhaps the most misleading of all. If 55 per cent of those questioned express themselves as satisfied with Presidential policy and 45 per cent as dissatisfied, one can say either that "the majority of the American people are pleased with President X—he is obviously doing his job" or that "almost half of the American people feel that President X is not doing his job properly. The dissatisfaction of such a large group is an obvious indication that something is seriously wrong in the White House." If you try hard enough, you can "prove" almost any preconceived notion with a set of statistics. For example, statistics show that most people who are sentenced to be electrocuted in the United States are black. That is a fact; it can be verified empirically. However, depending upon one's point of view, one can utilize the statistic to demonstrate that more murders are committed by blacks than are committed by whites and that blacks are more violent than whites, or that juries (usually predominantly white) which find white men guilty of murder are more likely to recommend mercy than they are in the case of black men, and that judges (usually white) are less likely to sentence white men to death. The factual statement remains constant; its interpretation, predicated on a value judgment, can vary widely from analyst to analyst.

Human beings cannot avoid making value judgments; they are part and parcel of our humanity and figure importantly among the devices that enable us to survive and prosper. If one of the functions of the political scientist is to involve himself in the workings of government, his estimates of which courses of action will be good or bad or valuable or harmful or desirable are necessary and welcome, because they are presumably based on knowledge and experience. If one of his functions is to teach, he must remember that mere collections of unorganized facts are not particularly useful to the student. It is up to political scientists to use their expertise to interpret the facts and make them meaningful. Unfortunately, interpretations may become confused with facts. Political scientists themselves must realize this and make it clear to their readers and audiences when they are reporting facts and when they are on the shaky ground of speculation and value judgments. Unless they are able to separate the two, political science cannot be very scientific.

Chapter 2

WHAT POLITICAL SCIENTISTS STUDY

Who acts politically

It may come as a surprise to students to learn that practically everyone in our society is involved in the political
process and acts politically at one time or another. Although we can characterize certain individuals or groups
who are always "in the political news" as political actors,
they constitute no more than the tip of an iceberg. The
bulk of the iceberg, not as obvious as the overt political
actors, consists of the groups for which the known actors

serve as spokesmen. It is groups that seek power and the ability to influence action through their spokesmen. Even individual politicians running for elective office would find themselves unable to do so if, behind them, there were not groups of people who feel that they will benefit—that their ideas will receive attention, that they will receive jobs, that in one way or another they will obtain a measure of power— from the candidate's success.

Almost everyone acts politically—or is a potential political actor —because everyone has certain needs and drives that he seeks to have satisfied. In our sophisticated society, these needs may be characterized as economic, religious, occupational, intellectual, or whatever. When individuals discover that they cannot satisfy their needs by themselves or through the smaller voluntary organizations they have created, they turn to the political arena. This is the genesis of all government, for government is one of the institutions established by men to do for them what they cannot do for themselves. It would be strange if men, having created government, and finding themselves unable to achieve their objectives through their individual efforts, did not turn to government for assistance. Government offers them not only the power to obtain whatever is desired but the force and authority of law and its great resources as well.

A man who seeks to alter broad national governmental policy affecting many people and groups does not simply walk into the appropriate government office and state his case. (If his problem entails the application of such a policy to a particular situation, of course, he will frequently deal directly and individually with the government. A citizen may very well present himself at the office of the appropriate governmental agency to complain about the hour of garbage collection in his neighborhood, or to inquire about the delay of his social security check, or to challenge the validity of the real estate tax assessment on his house. Here he is dealing with the government in its administrative rather than its policy-making function; that is, with those agencies that carry out the policies authorized by more powerful and more comprehensive bodies.) There are three major reasons for this. The first is that in a society of 200,000,000 people, the demands of one individual are not important enough to warrant the attention of the tremendous apparatus we call our government. The assumption is that a government that must tend to the concerns of 200,000,000 people cannot legitimately take the time and effort to deal with a minority of one.

This leads directly to the second reason for the lack of individual political action: In our country, made up of so many different people leading such diverse lives and enjoying so many different interests, it is practically impossible for a sane man not to find his needs and desires reflected in a good many of his fellow citizens. His place of residence, his occupation, his religion, his choice of recreation, his educational background—all will bring him into contact with people who possess the same characteristics and who consequently share similar interests and desires. A man who articulates his needs will quickly discover that many others feel as he does, and he will naturally band together with them in order to give his demands the greatest possible force.

Finally, individuals do not act singly in the political realm because the achievement of political power depends on manpower and organization. One man will probably not have all the talents necessary to the successful presentation of his demands. Thus use of the term "party" in referring to the Democratic or Republican party suggests a conglomeration of groups and individuals that have chosen to combine themselves within the framework of a large organization in order to gain authority and power.

Parties, however, are not the only political actors. They are made up of disparate groups that may, at various times and for various reasons, choose to act politically by themselves. These groups frequently do not label themselves as political and do not appear to be so on the surface. Corporations and unions are usually thought of as economic institutions. The American Medical Association and the National Education Association, for example, are generally looked upon as groups that are organized around particular occupational interests. It is axiomatic that the primary function of church groups is religious. Nevertheless, in our society, all of these groups play a political role.

Government in the United States is all-pervasive. This point will be discussed in greater detail later on. For the moment, it suffices to point out that government action can affect the activities and interests of all of the groups mentioned above. The involvement of government with business groups, for example, is historic. Most analysts will agree that one of the key stimuli to a government's establishment of stable relations with foreign countries is its desire to protect the interests of businessmen who wish to trade abroad. Today, the American government's decision to recognize a right-wing government in a Latin American country may mean that American corporation investments there will be safe, whereas its decision not to challenge the legitimacy of a Castro-type regime may mean the nationalization of all industry in that country and the concomitant loss of American corporations' assets. At home, the government's desire to raise corporate taxes is of concern to all corporations. Its extension of nationally enforced health or safety standards to various products necessarily affects corporations that produce such products. Similarly, labor unions are concerned when the government creates a wage-price index that determines the permissible limits of future raises or enacts legislation that requires unions to submit their contract disputes to binding arbitration. The American Medical Association's bitter fight against the enactment of Medicare legislation testified to the Association's belief that it was directly affected by government activity. The interests of the National Education Association are involved when the federal government decides to spend millions of dollars on education or when state governments pass laws forbidding public employees to strike. Religious organizations are affected financially by government agreement or refusal to help fund parochial schools or to tax church-owned property.

All of these groups have an interest in the actions taken by government. It would be naïve to expect them to sit idly by and do no more than watch the maneuvering over proposed legislation that will affect them. On the contrary, it can be expected that they will make concerted attempts to protect their own interests. It can be argued that if a corporation believes that a proposed government policy will hurt its profits, it has an obligation to its stockholders to attempt to change the government's mind, and that other groups have equal financial or moral responsibilities to their members. Whether one subscribes to this theory or views the organizations' actions as mere self-seeking or sees their activities as one of the ways in which various segments of the public contribute to meaningful political debate by making their positions known, it is undeniable that all such groups become political actors. Through lobbying, through members' appeals to their congressmen, through attempts to obtain broad public support, they seek to exert influence on the lawmakers and law enforcers. Not all groups are continuously active in the political arena; although some find so much governmental involvement in their spheres that they have permanent lobbyists, many are content to enter political life only on those sporadic occasions when they feel themselves to be immediately involved. Some, indeed, may have appeared likely to remain only potential political actors and may be rather surprised to find themselves involved in the political process. A bird-watchers society, for example, is not apt to be a political group at its inception; its main concern is the study and preservation of birds. However, should the group discover that a particular species is being shot down at such a rate that it faces extinction, the group is quite likely to decide that legislation is required to protect the blue-billed warbler or the red-spotted songster. It will therefore seek governmental action; in so doing, it will have changed almost unnoticed from an apolitical to a political organization. Thus, any group or individual is a potential seeker of political power and a potential factor in the political process. When events occur which individuals find deplorable, or when measures are proposed which they view favorably, they are likely to organize and act politically in order to achieve that degree of power and control over events that only the political process affords. Voters are political actors, although they may not think of themselves as such. It requires only an event about which he feels strongly enough to transform the voter into a more active participant in politics. Anyone who wants something in this world, whether it is to preserve the status quo or to change it, and who finds that the other institutions within society do not provide him with the relief he seeks, will sooner or later join the company of actors on the political stage.

How they act

Political action can take many forms. In general, any individual or group that undertakes action intended to influence the workings of the government is acting politically. The problem is that it is not always easy to discover whether the motivation behind its actions is truly political.

The method of political action chosen by a group depends to a great extent on the degree of political power it seeks. The aim of organized political parties is, in effect, to become the government: to put so many of its members into positions of power that it will have as much control over the governmental process as any one group can possibly hope to obtain. The methods utilized by parties are numerous and overt. They will appeal directly to the electorate through speeches, use of the mass media, door-to-door solicitation of votes, etc. They will attempt to influence public opinion and thus to gain votes. They will take frequent soundings of the voters, employing public opinion polls to discover what personal attributes and political views the electorate finds most appealing in a candidate. Such devices involve the employment of thousands of workers, paid and unpaid, and the expenditure of thousands and frequently millions of dollars.

The methods chosen also depend on the nature of the political system involved. Just as the strategy used by football or baseball teams is determined by the rules of the game, so political strategy is governed by the rules of the particular political system. In the United States, the President is elected by the people. Many voters insist on seeing candidates personally, and this desire, coupled with the enormous size of the country, results in the candidates' being subjected to long, arduous, and expensive campaigns. In Great Britain, the Prime Minister is in effect elected by the leaders of his parliamentary party. Citizens do not vote directly for him; as a consequence, parties concentrate on the elections of individual members of Parliament and the method of wide national exposure of one candidate is not utilized.

As a rule, interest groups do not seek political office, nor do they attempt to control all aspects of governmental policy. Their concern lies only with those policies that will affect them. Although such groups may appeal to the public to bring pressure on elected officials, their more usual approach is to lobby; that is, to work directly with the officials and bureaucrats who enact and enforce government policy, in the hope of influencing their decisions. This procedure enables them to avoid the expense and time entailed in attempts to influence public opinion. They do not seek to become the government, but rather to direct its actions.

There are exceptions to the rule that interest groups do not seek to put their own members into public office. In areas where one interest predominates over all others, the group that represents that interest may choose one of its number to stand for election. This might be true, for example, of a congressional district composed of practically no economic group other than tobacco farmers and the merchants who depend on their wealth. Most districts are either too large or too urbanized for this kind of one-interest candidate to be successful. It would be more likely for a strong interest group to seek out one of its members or a local citizen in sympathy with its aims and urge him to run with its support, on the understanding that he would have to adopt many positions unrelated to the group's aims in order to appeal to enough voters to assure his election. For this reason the candidate of a labor organization might well find himself soliciting the support of business. Even where such politically active groups attempt the realization of their goals through the election of their own personnel, they differ from political parties in the number of offices sought. No matter how strong or geographically broad the group, it will almost never run its own candidates for more than a few offices, and most of those will be local officials or national representatives of a small geographic area.

In general, interest groups are content to make their influence felt only on matters of direct interest to them. Even here, however, there are differences among groups. Very few, like the A.F.L.-C.I.O., may have originated as one- or two-issue organizations (in this example, their early interest was confined to such matters as improved hours and wages for working men) and gradually expanded their concern until they emerged as groups with such a broad range of interests that they now find themselves taking positions on practically every major governmental proposal or issue of the day. The A.F.L.-C.I.O. has widened its horizons so extensively in its attempt to protect all aspects of the life of the working man that it now takes positions on such matters as civil rights, air pollution, and federal aid to education. It boasts a very large membership, an extensive and efficient organization, and a permanent battalion of lobbyists.

A second category encompasses those groups that are large and broad but that tend to emphasize a smaller range of issues. The Chamber of Commerce and the various farm organizations are examples of such groups, one of whose primary functions is the political representation of their members. They can be differentiated from a third category of groups, like the various church organizations, which involve themselves in a variety of issues (aid to parochial schools, divorce and abortion laws, civil rights) but whose primary purpose remains nonpolitical and who therefore devote less of their resources to such political activities as lobbying. The American Medical Association might be placed in this category. This, of course, does not imply that such groups cannot be extremely effective on those occasions when they do choose to involve themselves in the political sphere, as is attested by the success of church groups in delaying and limiting abortion reform and of the A.M.A. in delaying the enactment of Medicare for twenty years.

Yet a fourth category comprises groups that focus on one major interest but which find that the nature of that interest occasionally thrusts them into a number of related areas. This is true of many of the civil rights groups, which argued that the war in Viet Nam was diverting funds needed in the civil rights struggle, and which therefore began to concern themselves with antiwar activities. Finally, there are one-issue groups that are relatively passive politically and that spring into political action only when their particular, highly specialized interest is at stake. Examples might be the sports associations, the Women's Christian Temperance Union, or the National Rifle Association.

The above categorization is based solely on frequency and extent of political involvement. Other categories might be formulated on the basis of size or effectiveness. Although both the Women's Christian Temperance Union and the National Rifle Association can be labeled one-issue groups, the size and effectiveness of the latter far outweighs that of the former. Mention should also be made of the infinite number of potential or temporary interest groups. Such groups come into existence to answer a specific need and are usually abandoned after the need has been met. A group of neighbors may organize themselves for political action if a series of traffic accidents has highlighted the need for a traffic light or if neighborhood feelings run strongly against the location of a proposed highway. Such groups may also appear in response to a geographically broader issue; for example, the Veterans Against the War in Viet Nam was conceived as an expression of sentiment against that war and may very well disappear once the war is ended. During the relatively brief period of their existence, such groups will act in much the same manner utilized by more permanent organizations: They may appeal to the public, but they will usually concentrate on bringing the pressure of numbers, strong interest, and potential votes to bear on government officials.

Voting is a form of political action, which is why one can say that most citizens act politically at one time or another. In addition, citizens may involve themselves in activities which are not designed to be political but which nevertheless produce political effects. An example of this might be the economically motivated decision of union members in a vital industry to go on strike. Although the workers may be interested only in higher wages or better fringe benefits, their action may well have political consequences. A lengthy strike in a key industry will create economic or security problems for the nation, and this in turn will lead to popular demand that the government act to settle the dispute. Government policy will become involved: Should the government insist on compulsory arbitration? Should it ignore its own wage-price guidelines in order to achieve a fast settlement? The actions that the government takes may later be endorsed or repudiated at the polls. Thus, acts of private citizens and groups, whose motivations were not political, may have such broad ramifications that they lead to alterations in governmental policy or in the composition of the government itself.

In the same way, seemingly nonpolitical actions taken by political figures may have political implications. An incumbent President who is expected to run for reelection within a year and who begins to follow a heavy itinerary of speeches to economic and occupational groups across the nation may claim to be doing no more than the obligations of his office require. It should be obvious, however, that a trip which will introduce him to potential supporters and contributors and which will gain wide publicity for the views he expresses has political overtones.

Consequences for political science

The great variety of political actors and actions is one of the factors that makes the task of the political scientist a complicated one. He must not only investigate and analyze political behavior, but he must also establish criteria for deciding what actions are political and who can legitimately be called a political actor. He will have to involve himself in trying to discover what visitors the President has, what contributions corporations made to what campaigns, which interest groups have enough loyal members of voting age to be of concern to governmental officials, what advertising companies are working out the best ways of projecting political "images." The methods used by political actors are as diverse and complicated as the actors themselves, and the political scientist must try to be aware of all of them.

Political science and the morality of politics

Politics is usually thought of in the United States as a dirty, corrupt, unsavory business practiced by rather vulgar, dishonest, and self-interested schemers. There are reflections of this belief in newspaper columns, folklore, and folk humor. Perhaps one of the oldest jokes concerning the morality of politics and politicians tells of a man, walking through a graveyard, who saw a tombstone inscribed "Here lies a politician and honest man." Unable to believe that the two traits could be found in the same individual, he commented, "There must be two people buried in that plot."

Although politics may not entirely deserve its unsavory reputation, that reputation stems in large part from a realistic assessment of politics as a struggle for power. Because politics is the struggle for power, and because political science is therefore necessarily the study of power and of those who seek and use it, it seems appropriate to ask why individuals and groups attempt to gain power and whether or not the search for and use of power is inevitably a dirty business.

The question is perhaps best approached by posing a companion question: What is power? What, exactly, is it that people in political life seek and extoll as the ultimate prize for political adroitness? The answer, simply stated, is: Power is the ability of one person or group to govern or influence the course of action to be taken by others. Possession of power implies that one person induces another to do something which the second person would not otherwise do or to act in a manner different from that which the second person would adopt if left to his own devices.

On the political level, power can be defined as participation in the making of decisions by political bodies. The greater the power possessed by a political actor, the more extensive his participation in decision making, so that ultimate power is explained as the absolute ability to determine what a decision will be. Absolute power, in the political world as elsewhere, is extremely rare; the struggle for power usually results in the obtaining of different degrees of power. Those who obtain the greatest degrees of power become political leaders; they may function either formally and visibly or informally and behind the scenes.

Political figures seek power in order to bring about legislation and policies they consider desirable. At one of his press conferences, the late President Kennedy was asked whether he liked being President, and when he answered in the affirmative, the next question posed was "Why?" The President responded by saying that the Presidency is where the power is. His answer is not to be misunderstood as an indication of megalomania or some evil desire to control other human beings. It represents, rather, his recognition that in order to achieve noble societal ends, in order to bring about that which one believes is best for one's country, one must have the wherewithal: the ability to determine and influence courses of action. This is power. Every group in society seeks it, either overtly, under such terminology as "black power" or "white power" or "Republican party," or covertly, as do the American Medical Association and labor unions and the National Council of Churches. All these groups seek power or influence in government in order to effectuate policies favorable to themselves. They turn their attention to the government in the knowledge that it can support its policies with vast resources and the threat of physical coercion. This does not necessarily mean that their purpose is a selfish one, although it may sometimes be so. Frequently, individual politicians or a group may sincerely believe that their ideas are best for the citizenry and that it is only through the implementation of those ideas that the population as a whole will be able to attain its goals. Thus, men may fight for power because they are interested in the good of the people and believe that their plans and ideologies will result in justice, liberty, material well-being, and the "good life."

It is equally true that, at any given moment in political history, one will encounter individuals who seek power purely for their own ends and who will resort to almost any means in order to obtain it. They will employ the formal mechanisms of political systems to achieve results opposed to those contemplated by the systems. Their primary interest may be economic or social or simply the sheer joy of exercising power arbitrarily.

This in no way negates the argument that power and the struggle for power is a necessary and inevitable aspect of political life. The recognition that a system may be misused from time to time does not obviate the need for that system. In itself, power is neither good nor bad; its coloration is derived entirely from its users. Government, like nature, abhors a vacuum; at any given moment, someone must be in power. The nature of the personalities and ideas of those in power will influence the future of the societies they govern. Without the ability of well-meaning men to influence the course of action, society can make no progress; without power, the best-intentioned men and the best ideas have no hope of success.

Politics, then, is not simply an immoral struggle for power, and political science is not merely an intellectualized account of the fray. Political science must not lose its objectivity, but neither can it be entirely valueless. It must examine all political movements and actors as honestly as possible, but it need not condone them all. Franklin Roosevelt, Adolf Hitler, Winston Churchill, and Josef Stalin all fought for power and exercised it at the same time, and yet it is obvious that not all of them exercised it for the well-being of mankind. Many political studies can rightfully claim to be meant as value-free analysis, in the sense that their authors do not attempt to pass judgment on the wisdom or desirability of the phenomena they are studying. Examples of such studies might be surveys of voting habits or examinations into the kinds of power exercised by congressional committees. On the other hand, political science as a whole must utilize its understanding of the political process in order to suggest what the goals of political action should be and how they can best be attained. It would certainly be strange for the branch of intellectual endeavor devoted to the study and analysis of politics to confine its pronouncements to mere journalistic reporting without offering the kind of advice that its familiarity with politics should make possible. Political science specializes in the examination of politics. Its practitioners are uniquely qualified to locate flaws and suggest alterations. That aspect of political theory which is devoted to the attempt to define the "good life" and the "just society" must be an ever-present element of political science.

Chapter 3

A FEW
BASIC CONCEPTS

Some concepts and ideas are so basic to the study of political science that they underlie all writing and discussion in the discipline. Unfortunately for the student, they are taken so much for granted that they frequently go undefined. It is the purpose of this chapter to introduce you to a few of them. Our selection is not entirely arbitrary, but it is necessarily limited, and we certainly do not claim that these constitute all the basic concepts with which you will have to become familiar.

The idea of *culture* was introduced earlier. It is the sum total of ways of living followed by a group of human

the

41

beings (a society) and transmitted from one generation to another. Modes and methods of living are derived from the necessity to develop a set of answers to the problems of living: the perpetuation and perhaps improvement of individual life; the allocation of power within a society; the relationships of the individuals within it. There would be no point to man's ability to transmit knowledge to other human beings if each man had to solve these problems for himself; human progress would be impossible. The solutions worked out by various men are therefore standardized and incorporated into the customs and institutions of a society and transmitted to subsequent generations.

Culture is an important concept in the understanding of man and the institutions he creates, for all men behave as they do partly because of the cultural environment that surrounds them from the time of their birth. This idea of the importance of culture to man's behavior is frequently referred to as the *culture concept*. It does not imply that human beings are no more than the sum of their culture. Every human being is unique, largely because of the genetic factors which play a primary role in determining his character and personality. The culture concept suggests the way in which the genetic uniqueness of individuals is filtered through their joint culture, so that personality is seen as being subtly altered by culture.

The key factor in the process of transmission of culture is *socialization*. This means that all human beings learn how they are expected to act through their interactions with other human beings. A child in Western society is taught that he is to drink from a glass and eat with a fork, that he is not to take other children's toys, that his selfishness is not permitted to operate beyond certain limits, that cleanliness is next to godliness. As a child, and later as an adult, he may wonder at the calm insistence of products of other cultures on eating with different implements—fingers, chopsticks, etc.—just as he may scorn the idea that all possessions should be shared or that cleanliness is not an overriding virtue. These emotions will result from the internalization of the standards he has learned through his interactions with other people. The standards will have become such an accepted and unconscious part of him that it will probably not occur to him to wonder if a fork is really the most efficient instrument for conveying food from plate to mouth (that is, the most efficient solution to the problem of how one will eat) or whether the concept of private property is the best or only possible solution to the problem of providing the individual with stores of food and clothing.

Socialization is a continuing process. The first few years of a child's life, when he learns so much about his culture, may hold more lessons in human behavior than all the subsequent years, but the process of socialization never really ends. It is carried on by the family, schools, the church, social and occupational groups, the mass media, etc. Driver education, the learning of an occupational skill and the behavior which is expected to accompany it, introduction to the roles of spouse and parent—all are elements of socialization. By the time the child is a few years old, he will have absorbed so many of the mandates of his culture that he will probably never be able to rid himself of it. This becomes increasingly true as the child grows older and his behavior patterns are reinforced through the praise or condemnation of the people around him. He may decide to reject his culture, but even his rejection will take clearly delineated cultural forms. An American may become a "hippie" in order to show his disdain for his society, but he will rarely put on a beggar's robes and wander through the countryside carrying a beggar's bowl. The dissatisfied Indian, on the other hand, is not likely to become a hippie. Thus, culture provides a sound basis for social relationships, for it enables all of the members of a society to know what behavior is expected of them and what they can expect of others.

Political relationships are one form of social relationships. As was indicated earlier, culture limits the choice of solutions to political problems to those that are societally acceptable. What would you think of the idea of an hereditary American Presidency, passed on from father to son? Does the idea strike you as ridiculous and perhaps ominous? Given their present-day culture, it would be inconceivable for Americans to adopt that particular solution to the problem of the distribution and transference of power. Your response to the idea is culturally conditioned. The hereditary kingships of the Middle Ages seemed entirely right and logical to the people who lived under them—and whose culture was very different from ours.

Political socialization—the inculcation of specific attitudes, be- and expectations about the political process—is carried on by a variety of agents. The earliest, obviously, is the family. Frequently, the child will hear his family discussing political matters. It is not surprising that he will quietly absorb many of their beliefs. More significantly, he will develop attitudes toward such matters as the nature of authority, the permissible limits of individual liberty, and the process by which decisions binding on all should be made by unconsciously noting how those matters are handled within the family. It is likely that he will eventually draw an analogy between family and nation and judge political events and his own political behavior by the standards of behavior followed by his family. The drawing of the analogy, of course, will be unconscious. In a similar manner, the child (and later the adult) will bring to the political process the lessons he has learned about authority and freedom and decision making from school, job, and other nonpolitical social organizations of which he may be a part. One cannot claim as a hard-and-fast rule that everyone who is raised by authoritarian parents and who attends authoritarian schools and who can boast of little or no autonomy or participation in decision making on the job will invariably subscribe to an authoritarian form of government, but the general relationship between socialization in nonpolitical institutions and political attitudes seems clear. Overt political teaching, in school as well as in the family, will also affect political beliefs: Dates and names studied in civics classes may be forgotten, but the underlying political ideology will be remembered. Overt inculcation of political attitudes may also be a function of higher education and of the mass media.

Socialization is the mechanism by which human beings learn and internalize the behavior patterns (roles) demanded of them by their societies. Viewed from another angle, the same process can be called *social control*. It is the means by which society maintains itself in a particular form. From the viewpoint of society, social control means that people are told to play certain roles and that certain behavior patterns are demanded of them. From the viewpoint of the individual, it means that he is conditioned by society to want to play those roles and to feel that he should follow those patterns. Social control, to put it somewhat differently, is the maintenance of social order: Everyone knows where he belongs and what he is expected to do. Social control of various kinds is maintained within the family, the school, church, the corporation, etc. Political science deals with the kind of social control that is maintained within the legal entity of the state. It examines the questions of who has political power (that is, who exercises social control in the political sphere), how they get it, how they keep it, how they use it, and, occasionally, how they lose it. Other social sciences investigate other aspects of social control and social power.

The existence of social control should not be taken to imply that societies are static and that patterns of influence and power do not change. There is probably no culture that is entirely static, although the rate of change varies from one to another. One might well ask how, if values are transmitted from generation to generation and institutions are the external manifestation of values, *social change* is possible. The answer is that unforeseen circumstances arise, creating new sets of problems that demand new answers. Such a circumstance arose, for example, with the abolition of slavery in the United States. It had been widely assumed that the status of ex-slaves would be resolved with the end of the Civil War. This, however, did not prove to be the case, for instead of one nation of free and legally equal men, the United States discovered that freed slaves were not truly equal. They neither shared the legal rights enjoyed by white Americans, nor possessed the same skills and access to opportunity. The new problem of whether to accept the idea of a society in which some men were less equal than others or to take positive action to ensure the true equality of all men gradually resulted in a general acquiescence in the less-equal solution. That solution is slowly being renounced, but the problem is still in the process of resolution and undoubtedly will continue to be so for some time to come. Once the unexpected consequence (unequal freed men) of a solution to an earlier problem (slavery) emerged, however, social change of one kind or another was inevitable.

Technological innovation also results in social change. Improvements in transportation and communication made possible a truly united United States far larger and more diverse than that envisioned by the Founding Fathers. The invention and perfection of the assembly line was partly responsible for the creation of giant interstate corporations and a new way of life for workers, which in turn resulted in societal demands for strong governmental bodies to regulate the corporations and alleviate the unhappy conditions of the working man. Geographical and physical factors can lead to social change: changes in climate or the exhaustion of supplies of particular foods or natural materials will create new problems. In addition, contact with different cultures plays an important role in social change. Different cultures have differing answers to the problems of social life. A society introduced to solutions unlike its own will begin to question the sacredness of its accepted answers and will usually find some aspects of the solutions of other societies which are intriguing or attractive or more efficient. The adoption of such new solutions, of course, is the essence of social change. Finally, all societies produce some individuals who, for still-unknown reasons of genetics or whatever, simply refuse to fit into the molds prescribed for citizens. Given sufficient intellect and zeal, they may produce the ideas and/or leadership necessary to persuade society to alter itself.

We have already seen that culture is a prime conditioner of the political process. The implication is that as social change occurs and the culture is altered, political change inevitably follows. This, in turn, reinforces the social changes and helps to perpetuate the new values. An instance of this can be found in the "Negro revolution" of the 1950's and 1960's. A whole plethora of social changes, which cannot be fully analyzed in a volume of this size, resulted in the demand by black citizens for greater equality of opportunity. The success of black Americans in organizing themselves and calling their demands to the attention of the entire nation was a major social change in itself. It led to political change: the registration of large numbers of Southern black citizens on voting rolls; the passage of the 1964 Civil Rights Act; the later passage of the 1965 Voting Rights Act and the 1968 Open Housing Act. These political changes reinforced and strengthened the new values of legal and at least partial economic equality of black and white Americans, for now the government insists that such equality be formally recognized. Political change thus legitimizes and institutionalizes social change. It says in effect that the society has accepted the new solutions and the new values implicit in the solutions, and that it considers both solutions and values so important that it is willing to put the great prestige and coercive power of the state behind

them. The new solutions are institutionalized, and the institutionaliza-
tion lends them even greater authority.

Social change leads to political change, and both frequently lead
to an alteration in the dominant *ideology*. An ideology is the body
of beliefs and myths and symbols shared by the citizens of a nation.
The American ideology, for example, includes among other facets the
beliefs that representative government is the best government, that
the state exists to serve the individual, that material success is a sign
of individual worth, that farmers are closer to the basics of life and
more worthwhile than members of other occupational groups, that
politics is a slightly dirty business, and that the American political
system is so superior that it should be adopted by all other nations.
Most ideologies are expandable; that is, they are broad enough to en-
compass a great deal of social change. The American ideal of individual liberty existed throughout the period of slavery, the years
following abolition, and the recent changes in the status of black
citizens. Our definition of liberty has been altered at various times
in our history, but our underlying belief that the word "liberty" represents a desirable ideal remains unchanged. On the other hand, the
early American insistence that the strongest governments should be
those geographically closest to the people—namely, state and local
governments—has been done away with by the twentieth-century
emergence of problems that demanded solution by a strong nation-
wide body and by the reluctance and inability of state governments
to deal with the problems of the cities. A portion of our ideology has
changed.

The ideology of a nation is related to its *political system*. A
political system consists of the governmental mechanisms that a society
creates in order to achieve the way of life it considers to be best, as
well as those private and semipublic associations that attempt to
influence the functioning of the formal governmental mechanisms.
City governments, county governments, state governments, the national government, Congress, the Presidency, the Supreme Court,
political parties, interest groups, primaries, elections—all of these
institutions or mechanisms are elements of the American political
system. The political system will change and expand as the society
changes and becomes more complex. The political system of a com-

plex society, in which the interrelations among people and their activities are numerous and varied, will mirror its multiplicity of roles and interests. Even a brief survey of American history will indicate that the political system established by the Constitution of 1787 is quite different from the political system of the second half of the twentieth century. Although most features of the 1787 system are still extant, many have been substantially altered, and many new elements have been added. The Electoral College, which was conceived of as an anti-democratic device by which a body of the wisest citizens would freely choose the President, has been converted into a rubber stamp that simply validates the choice already made at the polls. Political parties, primaries, and public opinion polls are all new political devices that have been incorporated into the original system. The alterations and additions constitute the reaction of the political system to the problems and challenges presented by social change.

Policy making is the process by which the government decides what its approach and response in various areas will be. The most familiar form of policy making is that found in legislatures, with their investigating committees, public hearings, floor debates, and recorded votes on proposed legislation. These are the outward manifestations of a complex procedure that may involve pressure brought by interest groups on legislators, campaigns to arouse and channel public opinion, the use of communications media by interested parties to influence both the public and each other, "deals" among legislators and between legislators and members of the executive branch, pressure on one side or the other exerted by the executive branch, etc. The making of policy entails the resolution of conflict: Different people and groups will want the government to do different things, and it is the struggle of each one of them to persuade the government to its point of view that constitutes the policy-making process. The final resolution of the conflict—the solution worked out to the societal problem involved—is embodied in the government's policy.

Policy can be made by executive officials, by judges, or by bureaucrats within the executive machinery. There are some areas of governmental action in which the President or governor or mayor is empowered to set policy alone, without formal legislative approval:

declaration of the existence of an emergency situation, recognition of a foreign government, etc. This does not mean that legislative officials are not consulted or that their opinions are not of major importance in the Executive's ultimate decision, but it does mean that the policy-making process is centered in the Executive and that it is he who decides upon the resolution of the conflict. Similarly, judges— and particularly those judges who sit on high courts, like courts of appeals or the supreme courts of the states and that of the nation— make and declare governmental policy each time they hand down a ruling on an issue of broad concern. (An easily understood example of this is the Supreme Court's 1954 ruling against "separate but equal" schools, which in effect declared that from that time on the policy of the national government would be to encourage the growth of educational integration.)

It is not as widely recognized by students that bureaucrats (civil servants and other administrators) also make policy and that they are one of the most important elements within the policy-making process. Every legislative and executive policy has to be carried out; this is why bureaucracies exist. Most policies, however, are spelled out in broad terms, so that they will cover a multiplicity of situations. It is up to the administrators to apply general policies to particular situations. This is the crux of their power. They can decide to make the enforcement process so slow or so inefficient that the announced governmental policy is totally ignored and the actual governmental policy as defined by the administrators is exactly the opposite of that enacted by the legislators or laid down by the Executive. Conversely, they can be so zealous in their implementation of a policy that it becomes even more stringent than originally intended. Knowing this, interest groups and lobbyists do not give up when they have lost or won a fight to influence the legislature. Instead, they carry the fight into the domain of the bureaucrat. Thus legislators, executive officials, judges, bureaucrats, interest groups, lobbyists, the public at large, the mass media, and various individuals all have a place in the policy-making process.

One final note about basic ideas: Throughout this book and throughout most writing in political science, the words "state" and

"nation" or "country" are used interchangeably. Although Americans
are used to thinking of a state as a kind of local subgovernment within
a larger federal government, this definition is peculiar to us and to
only a few other countries with federal systems. "State" traditionally
denotes "nation."

Chapter 4

APPROACHES TO POLITICAL SCIENCE

Subject divisions

Along with most other academic disciplines, political science is divided into a number of subject areas, although these areas overlap one another to some degree. They are separated primarily in order to organize a vast body of material into more workable units. Courses are formulated around these areas, of which there are usually four: American government and politics (replaced outside the United States by a study of the relevant domestic govern-

51

ment), comparative government and politics, international organizations and politics, and political theory.

The study of American government and politics deals with the political institutions most familiar to Americans: the Presidency, the Congress, the courts, political parties, interest groups, elections, state and local governments, administrative agencies, etc. It entails an examination both of the functions performed by the various institutions and of the dynamics by which they work. For example, in order to understand the Presidency, one must know what functions the President performs (Chief Executive, head of his party, Commander-in-chief, etc.) and how he operates (the bases on which he appoints major officials; the tactics he uses in trying to persuade Congress to enact his program, etc.). In studying political parties, one must consider both the functions of the parties (such as organizing the political campaigns which enable Americans to choose their leaders) and their behavior (how they choose their candidates; how they try to persuade the public to support them). Most political science departments offer a number of courses in American government, and some have more offerings in American government than in anything else. This is because it is easiest for us, as Americans, to understand the workings of governments generally if we begin with the one we know best. In addition, American government and politics is obviously the branch of political science with which the average American citizen most needs to be familiar.

Some political science departments may subsume courses in public administration, public law, and political parties, public opinion, and pressure groups under the general heading of American government. More extensive departments may treat each of these areas as separate categories. Whatever the organization, the content is relatively standardized.

The American federal bureaucracy has been called the fourth branch of our government. This is no more than a shorthand way of saying that many political functions are performed by the bureaucracy and that it exercises a good deal of political power. The study of public administration grew from a recognition that a branch of the national government—and of local and state governments as well— which employs millions of workers to perform tasks vital to the con-

tinued functioning of government is of sufficient importance to merit
investigation and analysis by political scientists. Courses in public
administration are concerned primarily with the "hows" of government rather than with the "whys." They deal with the structure and
tools of administrative organizations, with problems of financial administration, and with the human factors: personnel administration;
the relationships between bureau chiefs and employees; the relationship between the government and the citizen. Basically, such courses
look at the management of governmental affairs.

Courses in public law (constitutional law, administrative law,
jurisprudence) take as their subject matter the legal principles found
in a society and the institutions established to deal with them. They
focus on the courts both as purveyors of day-to-day justice and as
important actors in the policy-making process. They examine the
constitutional and political basis of law in a society; the organization
of the courts; the recruitment of legal personnel; the political ideology
which led to the development of and which is protected by particular
legal principles; the philosophy of law in any society; the attempt to
define such concepts as "ethics" and "morality" and "justice"; the
adjudicative role played by bureaucracies; the legal rights of citizens
and of different parts of the government.

The study of political parties, public opinion, and pressure
groups is an attempt to segregate and examine the dynamics of the
political process from its structures and institutions. It seeks to discover the forces that actually move the government, whether those
forces are economic, social, psychological, or ideological. It analyzes
the nature of propaganda; the ways in which public opinion can be
manipulated and measured; the role played in particular societies
by both political parties and pressure groups; the organization of
parties and groups; the techniques utilized by each; the reasons for
and attributes of political behavior; the way people vote and why.

Courses in administration, law, and the political process may
also be offered in a comparative context; that is, they may analyze
those areas of the political system as found in various countries as
well as within a particular one.

Courses in comparative governments and politics examine the
other nations of the world in the same way that courses in American

government examine our own political system. They inquire into a country's political institutions and behavior and frequently attempt to show how and why these are similar to and different from those of America and other countries. They also try to discover why particular countries adopt particular systems: Why did England develop into a constitutional monarchy while France is a republic and Switzerland chose an assembly form of government? What factors—social, economic, historical, religious, geographic—led to each choice? Answers may be given in survey courses covering varied geographic areas and political systems, in courses devoted to one country, or in courses that cover a specific part of the world, such as Europe, the Middle East, or Latin America. Comparative government also attempts to analyze the similarities and differences between developed (usually, Western) and developing or emerging (usually, non-Western) countries. It seeks to free thought patterns from the boundaries imposed by an examination only of Western political society and to discover methods of analysis that will be valid for all political systems.

Courses in international organizations and politics are concerned with the interrelations of the world's nations. The student of international politics will quickly realize that all nations of the world have dealings with other nations. All nations have a foreign policy and must deal not only with countries and ideologies that they find sympathetic but with those that are antipathetic as well. The student will study the types of organizations and policies that nations establish to facilitate those interrelations. He will examine institutions, such as the United Nations or the Organization of African Unity, and deal with such problems as why nations have much or little to do with each other, why they are at war or at peace, what standards and patterns they follow in dealing with each other, and what factors within a nation lead to decisions it makes affecting its relations with other nations.

The subject matter of political theory is the nature of political institutions, the theory of government, and the role that political leaders should play. Many political theorists are less concerned with the governmental institutions in existence than with those that should be in existence. Courses in political theory span both time and space by exploring the ideas of political theorists of many ages and as many nationalities. In studying writers such as Plato, Aristotle, Aquinas,

Machiavelli, Hobbes, Locke, Rousseau, Calhoun, Kant, Hegel, and Marx, the student becomes aware of the political institutions that existed in their times, the facets of those institutions these authors felt were good or bad, and the changes they suggested in order to make governments and men better able to serve their societies. Studying political theory will lead students to discover why it is that types of governments and political institutions considered desirable at one time may not be valid for the same societies at a later stage in their development. It will lead to such questions as, What makes democracy or monarchy desirable or undesirable, and what forms should they take? Why is it that different nations have different kinds of government, and is there one form that is best for all? What should a good law do, or a good leader? Each theorist has his own answer, incorporating his ideas of what life and human society are all about. The student may study individual theorists; he may compare theorists, noting the way in which one built upon the other; or he may try to draw connections between the theorists' societies and the models they proposed. He will search for the theorists' definitions of the good government and ask whether the definitions are still valid. He will also discover that political theory and political theorists did not end with these illustrious names, but that in modern life political theorists are still important in planning and implementing the type of government and society that will best satisfy present-day needs.

Another aspect of political theory as an intellectual endeavor is its investigation into the uses of political theories. Some theorists view most theories as a reflection of the attempts by political leaders to clothe their power with the trappings of legitimacy. Theories are seen as weapons in the struggle to obtain and retain power. "Theory" is used interchangeably with "ideology" and "propaganda" by these theorists, who devote themselves to an examination of the ways in which various theories have been used to serve the needs of political actors and of the impact theories have, in turn, on political contests. All political theories are bound to have important results in economic and social life as well as in the political arena. The Lockean theory of democracy as the involvement of government only in specified and limited spheres of action, for example, implies that the government should not trouble itself about the distribution of wealth, and that power in the economic realm should be allowed to fall to whomever can seize it. Thus, Locke's theories might be viewed as an ideological justification of a particular economic system—or, at the least, as having the effect of justifying that system. Some courses in political theory will therefore be addressed to an analysis of the utilization of different sets of doctrines for the purpose of legitimizing and justifying the exercise of power by particular groups, and of the substitution of propaganda for outright physical coercion as a method of social control.

These, then, are the four major divisions of the discipline known as political science. Now imagine for a moment that you are taking a course in one of these areas. Suppose that you are in an introductory course in American government, and you are trying to understand the relationship between the President and the Congress. You have learned that in every recent year the President has submitted to Congress a bill allocating funds for foreign aid to a number of countries and that each year Congress has given the President only a portion of the money he has requested. You have been told that this issue has resulted in an annual struggle between the President and Congress, and you want to know why. You vaguely remember an indignant congressman glaring through your television screen and proclaiming his intention of fighting to the last breath against the strewing of bundles of American dollars to reckless foreign winds. What is it all about? Obviously, you must find out what foreign aid is, why we have given it in the past, why the President feels it is useful, why the congressman feels it has been wasted, what has happened to it once it has reached foreign lands, and why both President and Congress consider it to be such an important issue. Among many other things, you discover that one of the arguments made for foreign aid is that if America doesn't give it to economically needy nations, some of them may turn for aid to the Russians or the Chinese or whomever. Well, you ask, why should that make a difference to us? And suddenly you find that you are in the area of international politics. What, you ask, really will happen to the Congo or Bolivia or Thailand if they don't get American aid? And suddenly you have left the United States and are enmeshed in the economic problems of the emerging nations.

This description of an imaginary inquiry is not meant to discourage you from ever undertaking any political investigation. It is designed to show that the category divisions within political science are somewhat arbitrary. You cannot fully comprehend why Jefferson and Hamilton came to symbolize two different views of American government unless you know their ideas of what a good and beneficial government should do and their views of the then-current world situation—or, to put it differently, the study of American government cannot be entirely complete without the study of political theory and international politics and comparative government. These areas cannot possibly be examined all at once, and so for the sake of the learning process political scientists differentiate among them and take them one at a time. It should be remembered, however, that they are mutually complementary parts of a whole. Knowledge in one area will help you in another; for example, familiarity with different forms of government will aid your understanding of the choices that were open to the United States and the factors that went into the decision of what form its government was ultimately to take. A competent political scientist must have some proficiency in every area.

Similarly, your foray into the problems of foreign aid will have shown you that political science cannot be divorced from economics. Before you can evaluate the wisdom of foreign aid policy, you must consider the impact of various kinds of aid on both the American and the recipient economies. If you want to know why Congress passed a tax law or why poverty is such an explosive political issue, you will run up against economics again. A discussion of why Americans vote as they do will take you not only into economics and sociology but into religion and psychology as well. Once more, you will discover that the social sciences are inextricably interrelated, and that it is only to facilitate study that they are treated as separate categories.

Further proof of the interrelationship of political science with the other social sciences is found in the relatively recent creation of area studies programs at a number of universities. Such programs involve the joint participation of many people, such as political scientists, economists, sociologists, anthropologists, and historians who specialize in the study of areas of the world (such as Asia, Africa, etc.) or individual countries (China, the Soviet Union).

Methodologies

Students sometimes think of Truth as a great secret, entrusted to select wise men and professors, which is nevertheless available to anyone who will take the trouble to read, outline, and commit to memory all of the items on his reading lists. It therefore comes as something of a shock to discover that few professors can agree about what belongs on a reading list, much less about what constitutes Truth.

Reading lists for the same course vary from college to college and from section to section within the same college because different professors have different methods of approaching their disciplines and tend to weight their lists with the books of those writers whose approach agrees with their own. There is no one unanimously accepted approach to political science. The present authors lean toward an eclectic method that incorporates some of the features of various approaches. Adherence to this method is based on the belief that a political science that confines itself to one technique must necessarily be incomplete. This approach, however, is unacceptable to many of the exponents of the two major methodologies, functionalism and behavioralism, currently favored and argued about by political scientists. It should be understood that the approach utilized in this book is far from the only one possible and represents a choice on the part of the authors.

As its name implies, functionalism concentrates on the political functions performed by people and institutions. It asks, for instance, what Congress does (enacts legislation, declares war, ratifies treaties, etc.) and what congressmen do (introduce legislation reflecting the wishes of their constituents, serve on legislative committees, etc.). But functionalists go beyond the facade of formal governmental institutions and simple textbook descriptions of who does what. They are concerned with determining who in fact wields power; for example, which congressmen have the greatest influence on policy making, even though theoretically every congressman has an equal vote. The functionalist will discuss the power the chairman of a congressional committee wields in the making of laws and the power he wields in fighting for or against a President. In the final analysis, the functionalist will take the basic, formal structure of government and attempt to discover who within it actually has power, how much, and how it is used. Thus, for example, the functionalist will argue that although all congressmen are equal, some are more equal than others. He will therefore examine both the ideology of a nation and the workings of its political institutions in order to ascertain the nature of its political system.

Rather than concentrate on the behavior of individual members of society (unless, of course, those members occupy high office or are uniquely important to the political process in some other way), the functionalist will, for the most part, give preference to the analysis of continuing systems of activities and persistent patterns of action and organization found among groups and within the society as a whole. He may, on the other hand, draw conclusions from intensive examination of one action. He relies less on quantity of raw material than on his ability to construct generalizations from his observation of the entire political process or parts thereof at work.

A relatively new approach to political science, which may be included under functional methodology, is the systems analysis approach. This technique has been derived primarily from the attempts of comparative political scientists to suggest a valid basis for the description and comparison of political institutions in both Western and non-Western societies. One of the discoveries made by analysts of non-Western societies is the extent to which institutions not usually thought of as political in the Western world may play important political roles in the cultures of the developing nations. Primary political roles, for example, may be played by kinship groups (families), status groups, occupational groups, etc. Thus analysts began to realize that there is a great deal of interdependence between political and non-political life, and that "nonpolitical" structures may be of considerable political significance.

Gradually, therefore, these analysts have begun to develop the idea of the political system as basic to any analysis of any society. They see the political system as including all institutions that play political roles, but at the same time they recognize that institutions may play nonpolitical roles that are not part of the political system or of the domain studied by the political scientist. For purposes of analysis, then, they have come to rely on the concept of political function rather than on that of political structure. They ask what political functions are performed in all societies, and then they are able to move to a consideration of the institutions or structures that perform them. One political function might be the application of particular rules, or policies, to different situations and people. A systems analyst may see rule application in the United States as being done by the various bureaucracies, the courts, and, occasionally, by the legislatures. He may see the rule-application function in a Latin American country as being performed by high executive officials, the bureaucracies, the courts, and the church. Courts in the United States also perform the functions of making rules and of adjudicating them; legislatures also make rules, and so on. Systems analysts have thus come to insist on the importance of the concept of multifunctionalism; that is, the realization that structures or institutions may perform a number of different kinds of functions and that a variety of institutions may perform the same function with differing degrees of intensity and influence.

The idea of the political system is a useful artificial construct that draws boundaries between political and nonpolitical activities for the purpose of analysis. The study of family life, for example, is left to psychologists and sociologists—except where one family dominates politics, as in Nicaragua, or where the analyst is examining such political activities of the family as political socialization. Various systems, such as economic, social, and religious systems, are not studied as such by the political scientist. The political system is distinguished from other systems within the society, even while it is understood that it is related to the others. Integration among the systems is not complete, however, so that a change in one does not invariably cause corresponding changes in the other.

Both functionalists and systems analysts study the performance of political functions with the understanding that the form of the institutions playing political roles may limit the extent and nature of their functioning. A policy will differ in form and probably, therefore, in content, depending upon whether it is enunciated by Congress, with its relative freedom to frame laws in any way that it wishes, or by the Supreme Court, which is restricted by the need to follow established legal formulas in announcing new decisions. Functionalists and systems analysts agree, however, that the study of nothing more than the forms of institutions cannot adequately explain the functions played by them. Congress is the only national body formally organized to make laws, but it is undeniable that the President, the Supreme Court, the parties, interest groups, etc.—all of which are formally designed to fulfill other functions—play vital roles in lawmaking. In short, functionalists and systems analysts retain an awareness of form but go beyond it to concentrate on function.

Behavioralists concentrate less on the workings of governmental institutions than they do on the workings of individuals and groups. Knowing that all political institutions are made by men and given motion by individuals acting in certain ways, they argue that one cannot understand the institutions without first examining the behavior of the individuals who compose and comprise them. Before turning to the question of how the Senate functions, they will ask why it is that individual senators and groups of senators behave in certain ways in exercising their legislative function. Behavioralism is greatly concerned with the inevitable human aspect of political institutions. The object of their inquiries is the discovery of patterns in the actual behavior of individuals and groups. They tend to concentrate on relatively narrow areas of inquiry so that the subjects under consideration can be examined empirically and so that their findings can be easily and repeatedly verified. This has led to the use of modern mathematical and computer techniques in compiling and sorting huge quantities of data about how people—for example, voters, judges, congressmen—have behaved. It is in the choices that people have made that behavioralists seek to discover what their politics is all about.

Behavioralism emphasizes description rather than prescription. It is an attempt to avoid the formulation of "oughts" by defining the realm of legitimate inquiry as that which can be proven and reproven through the use of the most neutral and nonsubjective techniques available. Behavioralists are extremely wary about offering broad laws and tend to utilize "hypotheses" rather than "generalizations." They produce analyses of voting behavior, decision making, the formation of political opinion, the behavior of political elites, and, particularly, the functioning of groups. The examination of groups is seen as the best way in which to understand the nature of power, since groups are organizations designed to achieve power and can therefore be perceived as being among the basic units of political life. It is a prime aim of behavioralism to reduce data to basic units of behavior that can be observed and described in empirical terms.

Functionalists may deal with broad, complex areas; behavioralists prefer smaller, more discrete problems. Functionalists concern themselves with institutions, structures, and functions; behavioralists with behavior and roles. Functionalists both describe political activity and suggest what it should be; behavioralists usually confine themselves to descriptions of political behavior as it actually exists. Functionalists derive many of their tools from philosophy and history; behavioralists, from psychology and mathematics. As you will discover in the course of your studies, individual political scientists strike variations on these themes, so that not all behavioralists will view political science in the same manner, and functionalists will differ on the value of behavioral analysis of political phenomena.

Both functionalists and behavioralists are searching for the truth, which seems to be an extremely elusive entity not necessarily recognizable upon discovery. It might be interesting, after having read your political science assignments, to see whether you can tell in which direction any given author leans. This exercise should not divert you from digesting the material, but it could give you some insight into political science as a human endeavor.

Chapter 5

USES OF
POLITICAL SCIENCE

"What is Government 101 (or Botany 314 or Music 5) to me?" Probably every student has wondered on occasion what he is doing in a certain classroom and what the professor's lecture has to do with him, as he finds himself suspended somewhere between high school adolescence and the "real" world.

A course is not justified by the mere fact that it is a part of the curriculum. Presumably, you are required to take certain courses or are permitted to select them because they will be of value to you. Courses in political science, along with those in other disciplines, are offered because of this presumed value. What, specifically, does political science have to offer you?

Obviously, someone who is considering a career in politics or public service should have some idea of what it is he is getting into. Here, as in other areas of life, no set of classroom lectures can fully prepare him for the nonacademic world. Studying political science is not a substitute for experience in political life, nor is it meant to be. Rather, the function of political science for the would-be politician is to equip him with a general outline of his future environment. It will familiarize him with the basic entities of the political system in which he hopes to function and will indicate the possibilities and limitations that will confront him. It will acquaint him with the organizational charts and written documents and tell him how political agencies and groups actually behave in carrying out their stated functions. Later on, when he is actively functioning in the political world, he will be able to fill in further details for himself. As a start, however, the study of political science will give him a key to the world he expects to enter. It will introduce him to the ideas and questions that are a vital part of that world.

The proportion of students who choose politics as their profession is relatively low. The question of the value of political science for the nonpolitician remains. To answer it, we must consider the average student both as a citizen and as a thinking animal.

Today's Americans are commonly depicted as alienated masses, pushed about by an automated world they do not understand, reacting with apathy, and filled with a vague sense of things not being quite right. It is nevertheless the same Americans who go to the polls every two years to elect their congressmen, read thousands of words about politics in their newspapers every day, and exercise their time-honored right to grumble about "the bums in office" and the lack of honest men in the halls of government. Americans may feel remote from the centers of decision making, but unless they close their eyes to the eleven o'clock news and shut their ears to the conversations around them, they are part of the political world. Indeed, if they refuse to be part of it, there can be no political world, for no one in the United States but the citizen has the power to choose the government. Only the mass of citizens can elect a President every four years or decide the composition of the Senate. Interest groups may fight for various causes, and politicians may huddle and orate, but the ultimate power to grant a man political office or deprive him of it rests with the people. How appalling, then, to contemplate a nation of political innocents, devoid of any knowledge of the political process, not having a basis on which to decide whether a policy is practical or a politician wise, nevertheless placidly and ignorantly endorsing or destroying those policies and politicians! Were such a situation to exist, one might call our system rule by peaceful mobs rather than a democracy.

To avoid such a nightmare, citizens must have some knowledge of the workings of the government. This does not mean that they can confine themselves to domestic affairs. In an era when the government is heavily involved in foreign policy, a rudimentary understanding of other governments and of international affairs is necessary before the citizens can evaluate their own. Familiarity with the "oughts" of political theory is similarly required. In order to meet no more than the simplest demands of citizenship, then, one must have at least a passing acquaintance with the teachings of political science.

Citizens are not only the subject of government, however; they are its object as well. The influence and effect of federal, state, and local governments on American life is so pervasive that no citizen can remain untouched by it. The college you are in is directly affected by the government: Laboratories and dormitories may have been built partly at government expense; faculty members may be doing research financed by government grants; you or your fellow students may have government scholarships or government-backed loans. The telephone you use is government regulated, many of the foods you buy are government inspected, the car you drive must adhere to government safety standards, the bus you take may be government-run, the streets you use are government property. If you are not now eligible for that particular frustration, you will someday find part of your income going to the government; indeed, you are already paying excise or sales taxes on some of the things you buy. If you are a man, the chances are that the government will demand two years or more of your time; in wartime, the government may even require you to sacrifice your life.

The important point here is that government in every industrialized, urbanized society, including the United States, is ubiquitous. Its effects are pervasive and inescapable. Whether or not the citizen chooses to take an interest in his government, it is interested in him. It has the power to establish the rules that will govern major portions of his behavior and his interrelationship with those around him. It would thus seem logical for the citizen to ask himself not only why the government plays such a dominant role in his life but whether he is satisfied that its aims and means are legitimate.

Much of what you "learn" in college you will forget shortly after you graduate—if, indeed, you do not forget part of one semester's lessons by the beginning of the next. So much information in so many different areas of knowledge is crammed into so little time that it is probably impossible for anyone to remember all of it. Of course, there are many things that you will remember, either because you found them particularly interesting or useful, or because they were exceptionally well taught. It has already been suggested, as an example, how important it is for citizens to retain some of their lessons in American government.

Colleges undoubtedly fill an essential community need in their capacity as repositories of information and knowledge. For the individual student, however, this is secondary. There are certain things that he must know in order to function in our world, and college will teach him some of them. If his college years do no more than fill him with quantities of information which he may or may not forget, however, their value seems questionable. This is not meant to imply that there is no point in trying to learn specific facts in college on the grounds that they will all eventually be forgotten anyway. In the course of absorbing specifics, students unconsciously acquire approaches to the world of the intellect as well as important general knowledge of a variety of fields. Certainly, the most important of these approaches is the broadest: the methodology of problem solving.

The one lesson of permanent value that can be taught in college is how to think. Man's intelligence is one of the major characteristics that distinguishes him from other animals, but most human beings do not come equipped with the techniques necessary to make the most of their intelligence. They do not know how to apply it to the problems they face. Just as an infant must learn how to manipulate another amazing human instrument, the hand, in order to give his spoon and its contents some chance of landing in his mouth, so must his elders learn to use their minds in order to solve the more abstract problems of adulthood. If the goal of the college is to produce well-rounded and informed individuals capable of leading full, creative lives, then its primary means must be to teach its students to think.

Political science is a discipline particularly well suited for this task. The subject matter with which it deals changes constantly as new personalities, events, and institutions make their appearance on the political scene. Even while a student is working through a course in American government or international relations or comparative government, current events in those subjects demand his attention. He must accustom himself to applying the problem-solving processes he has mastered to the new situations, and in turn the current events help to illuminate the basic material he is trying to learn. No textbook can tell him what his analysis of a governor's or a president's actions ten years hence should be, but it can enable him to perceive the method he should use to analyze any political executive's actions at any time.

This constant interaction between life and theory is one of the things that can make the study of political science extraordinarily exciting. More significantly, it benefits the student who is trying to learn how to think: It helps him to discern the relationship between the knowledge stored in his brain and the events of the outside world. It shows him how to approach the analysis of problems on a day-to-day basis. If he has acquired that skill, his education has been very much advanced.

Chapter 6

HOW TO STUDY POLITICAL SCIENCE

Students are usually required to perform three basic tasks in any introductory political science course, beyond attending lectures and participating in discussions: reading texts, taking exams, and writing papers. We shall assume that exams in political science are not radically different from exams in other areas and that you have some elementary knowledge of how to go about taking them, and we will confine ourselves here to a discussion of reading texts and writing papers.

Most students approach required reading with pen and notebook in hand, assuming that their major problem is one of logistics: how to reduce hundreds of pages of print into as few pages of notebook as possible. The legitimacy of the reading is never questioned: The teacher assigned the book and so it is important. It may be dull, it may be difficult to comprehend, it may be too long, it may be thoroughly frustrating—but the teacher assigned it and no matter how awful it is, it is also important. In truth, however, the most intriguing thing about a book is not that it has become assigned reading, but that someone took the trouble to write it. Someone sat down and did all the research and all the thinking and all the organizing and then all the laborious writing and rewriting that goes into the making of a book. And although very few students ever take the time to wonder why an author chose to go through all that labor, the answer is also the key to the way in which they ought to read this book.

Anyone can write a book, and the fact that it is published does not necessarily mean that it is worth anybody else's time. The books that appear on your reading list, however, have been chosen out of hundreds of possibilities by an instructor who is an expert in his field. You can assume, then, that the books are worth reading and merit your attention because they deal with something that your instructor thinks you should know. It can also be presumed that this feeling is shared by the author: He believes that what he has to say is worth writing about. Your primary assignment is to find out what it is.

Unless he is writing a monograph devoted to the clarification of the specific date on which an event occurred, an author does not usually write hundreds of pages merely to set off a variety of dates. His main concern is not to string together a series of disconnected facts. He is trying to make a point; this is his reason for writing a book. He may need to introduce facts and dates in order to illustrate or prove his thesis, but it is the thesis that is the reason for the book's existence. There is little point, for example, in his telling you that Mr. X was President of the United States in such and such a year unless he uses this fact to illustrate a particular idea, such as that any President in office during that year would have found himself forced by circumstances to do certain things and that a President is not entirely a free agent but is limited in the exercise of his discretion by various events and other factors; or, conversely, that President X had a number of choices and that his actions changed the course of American history.

What we are dealing with here is the relationship between facts and generalizations, or between data and ideas. Obviously, generalizations will not mean much to you unless you understand the facts on which they are based, but you should not forget that it is the generalizations—the interpretations of facts, the ideas—that matter. You must walk before you can run; you must assimilate a good many facts before you can go on to generalizations. Nevertheless, you must remember that much of political science is devoted to the analysis of political institutions and events, and although those institutions and events constitute its basic material, one of its major purposes is analysis. Political science is part of the study of human behavior. It may be interesting to know that particular human beings behaved in a certain way at a certain time, but it is both interesting and instructive to discover why they did so or to postulate that given certain circumstances they will do so again. Political science, it was suggested earlier, is less an accumulation of "whats" than of "hows" and "whys."

To prove this to yourself, and to experiment with a note-taking technique that you may find valuable, take a chapter in any of your readings and skim through it. Read it quickly, concentrating on discovering the gist of the matter: the ideas, the generalizations, the interpretations. Now take a sheet of paper and begin an outline. Write down the name of the chapter you are outlining, and then your first heading. The heading should summarize the first major point of the chapter: "Political parties are organizations of individuals and groups who seek to gain control of the government through the electoral process" or "The conflicting ideas of Hamilton and Jefferson set the basic categories of American political discussion." Now read the chapter carefully, putting explanations or important facts in subheadings: "The methods used by political parties are . . ." or "Hamilton's major ideas were . . . ," etc. As you go through the chapter add the prominent ideas you find. Your outline will then look something like this:

```
I. The conflicting ideas of Hamilton and Jef-
   ferson set the basic categories of American
   political discussion.
```

A. Hamilton's ideas:
  1. Strong central government in the
     hands of the wise and the able.
     a. Purpose: to prevent control by an
        uninformed populace.
        1) Note: distrust of the average
           man.
     b. Close alliance between the gov-
        ernment and commercial interests.
        1) Reason: Commercial interests
           are the most powerful. They can
           destroy the government. Must
           believe that their interests
           will benefit from the govern-
           ment's existence.
           a) Importance of government
              of laws rather than of
              force: anarchy the great
              enemy.
        2) Reason: importance of rule by the
           propertied interests.
           a) Inevitability of a propertied
              aristocracy.
  2. The United States should be commercial,
     urban, industrialized.
     a. _____
     b. _____
  3. Most important: Government must be
     stable.
     a. _____
  4. _____
  5. _____
B. Jefferson's ideas:
  1. The strongest governments should be those
     closest to the people.
     a. Centralized government will lead to
        rule by the few.
     b. Importance of a true democracy.

2. Government should be basically negative.
   a. _____
3. The United States should be primarily
   agrarian.
   a. Cities seen as evil.
      1) _____
   b. _____
4. It is more important that government be
   just than that it be stable.
   a. _____
   b. _____
C. Basic categories of American political
   discussion.
   1. _____
   2. _____

The partial outline above is neither meant to be complete, nor designed to be the definitive exposition of Hamilton and Jefferson's ideas. It is simply an example of how you might go about doing your reading and note-taking: Make sure that while you do not lose sight of the facts, the overall generalizations receive the bulk of your attention. You have found out what Jefferson's ideas were, but this remains no more than a disconnected piece of data unless you can connect it with the larger problem of American political thought in his day. The author's objective in writing the chapter will also have become clear to you: He wants to show the differences in Hamilton and Jefferson's ideas and the ways in which those differences became the rallying points for political factions.

Whether or not you adopt the outline approach in your reading, its basic purpose remains valid: Look for broad ideas and don't clutter up your notebook with a mass of unrelated facts. You should be able to compress most chapters into two or three pages of notes; if you go much beyond that limit, reread what you've written and see if you haven't done some unnecessary scribbling. Once you have gained some practice in the outline method—should you choose to use it— you ought to be able to go through readings only once, outlining as you go. And one suggestion: It might prove worth your while to go over your lecture notes in the evening, rewriting them and putting them in outline form. That way, at the end of the semester, you will have organized lecture and reading outlines from which to study.

Research papers

Writing a research paper in political science is very much like writing such a paper in the other social sciences or the humanities. You begin with a topic and a tentative outline. If the subject you are researching is totally unfamiliar to you, the outline can wait until you have read one or two general books on the topic. It should not wait much longer than that, however, or you are liable to waste time accumulating notes that will later prove to be irrelevant.

Once you have organized an outline, your next problem is a bibliography. You must decide where you will look for material. Your first reference can be found in a variety of ways: It may be recommended by your instructor, it may have been mentioned by the authors of one of your textbooks, it may be suggested by a librarian, or you may simply have come across it in the card index at the library. The next step is to see what further sources the author of your first book lists in his bibliography as shedding light on your topic. Presumably, his reading has been much broader than yours, so he should be familiar with most of the work in the field. You should know how deeply your paper must probe so that you will be able to decide whether secondary sources will be sufficient or whether you will have to utilize original sources.

Your topic may involve events so recent that books have not yet been written about them. Your first step in that case might be to search the *New York Times Index,* which lists all the articles published in that newspaper under appropriate subject headings and under the names of the individuals involved, or *Facts on File,* which summarizes current events. The British *Annual Register of the World's Events* is published yearly and may be of some use to you. Next, you might go to the *Reader's Guide to Periodical Literature* and the *Social Sciences & Humanities Index,* formerly the *International Index to*

Periodicals, both of which index recent articles in magazines, and to the *Public Affairs Information Service Bulletin,* a monthly index which concentrates primarily on articles about the social sciences published throughout the English-speaking world. The *American Political Science Review,* published quarterly by the American Political Science Association, contains articles and book reviews. Each December issue includes an index to all of the articles and reviews of the past year. Important articles are also to be found in the *Public Opinion Quarterly,* published by the Princeton University School of Public and International Affairs; in the bimonthly *Annals of the American Academy of Political and Social Science;* and in *Foreign Affairs,* which appears four times a year. The *Congressional Quarterly Service* summarizes major events within the American government. It is issued weekly, with cumulative 90-day indexes and a yearly Almanac. It also publishes periodic reports on selected topics such as civil rights and federal aid to education.

Besides the accumulation and note-taking of the substantive material you need for your paper, there are a few things you should do as your reading progresses. Be sure to write down the complete title, author, publisher, and date of the sources you use. You will need this information for your bibliography. Make a note of the page number whenever you copy a passage in the author's words; if you are going to quote him, you must cite the page number in your footnote. Make a similar notation whenever you think a footnote might be necessary: when the author presents a not generally known fact or delineates a particularly controversial or highly individual opinion. Remember that footnotes, used in moderation, do not indicate a lack of thought on your part. A beginning student cannot be expected to come up by himself with all the cogent thoughts possible on what is, to him, a relatively unfamiliar subject. Footnotes show that you have sought out and chosen among the assertions of those more cognizant of the problem than yourself. For clarity and completeness the following system of footnoting is recommended:

For a book:

(1) Author's name as it appears on the title page

(2) Title (underscored)
(3) Place of publication
(4) Publisher
(5) Date of publication (use date on copyright page)
(6) Volume (if any) and page number

³ John Smith, <u>Congresses and Parliaments</u> (New York: A. B. Clark & Co., 1966), p. 36.

For a magazine article:

(1) Author's name
(2) Title of article (in quotation marks)
(3) Name of magazine (underscored)
(4) Volume or number
(5) Month and year of publication
(6) Page number

⁶ John Smith, "How Congresses and Parliaments Differ," <u>American Political Magazine,</u> Vol. 8 (July, 1967), p. 413.

Items (4), (5), and (6) may be shown as follows:

VIII <u>American Political Magazine,</u> 413 (July, 1967).

For a reference to a work cited in the immediately preceding footnote, and if the reference is to the same place in the same work, use:

⁹ Smith, <u>ibid.</u>

If the reference is to a different page in the same work, show:

¹⁰ Smith, <u>ibid.,</u> p. 39.

If you are referring to a work a second time, but other works have been footnoted between the first and second mention, show it as follows:

¹² Smith, <u>op. cit.</u>

If the page number varies from the previous reference, it should be shown:

```
16 Smith, op. cit., p. 67.
```

Your bibliography should include the same material you put in your footnotes; for books, page numbers are omitted. Authors are listed alphabetically, last name first.

The way in which you organize your note-taking is up to you. You may prefer to allocate separate index cards to different sources or to take continuous notes on a loose-leaf pad. The thing to remember is that you can always choose later not to use material which seemed important at the time, but it is a nuisance and sometimes impossible to relocate the source of a passage which sticks in your mind but that you didn't bother to write down.

You may write a first draft of your paper and decide to do some additional research, or you may feel that your draft covers unnecessary ground and that you can eliminate some sections. After you have written a paper or two you will know something about your technique and what changes in it may be advisable. One word of warning: Keep your notes and your rough copies until your paper is graded and returned. It might even be wise to make two copies of your final draft and retain one. It doesn't happen frequently, but papers can go astray, and it would be unpleasant at the very least to find yourself doing all your research over again.

Day-to-day research

As a student of political science, you ought to be aware of the political events taking place at the very time you are pursuing your studies. No professor, however inspiring, and no book, however brilliant, can hope to be a substitute for your own view of politics in action. You will gain an infinitely better understanding of politics if you can watch the political process at work. The easiest and most efficient way to do this is to read a good daily newspaper. The *New York Times,* the *Los Angeles Times,* the *Washington Post,* and the

St. Louis Post-Dispatch are outstanding examples of American newspapers with wide coverage of politics at home and abroad. If you feel
that your local newspapers are unsatisfactory, perhaps you will find
that one of the above is available in your area. Weekly news magazines
and journals of opinion are also useful. News magazines such as *Time*
and *Newsweek* sometimes purport to be objective, although they are
not; journals of opinion usually do not make the claim and never live
up to it. The spectrum of American political opinion is represented
by journals, from *The Nation* and *The New Republic* on the left
through *The Atlantic* and *Commentary* to the *National Review* on the
right. (These are only a few titles out of a great variety.) All magazines and newspapers should be read with the thought firmly in mind
that no matter how objective they may seem on the surface, they
possess underlying philosophies that necessarily color their reports.
You can gauge your reading sophistication by your success in discovering each publication's particular form of bias.

Chapter 7

VOCATIONAL OPPORTUNITIES FOR THE STUDENT OF POLITICAL SCIENCE

A background in political science is not like a background in accounting or architecture—it does not prepare the student for a specific career. Majoring in political science in college does not, of itself, constitute a sufficient introduction to the skills necessary in most jobs open to college graduates. What college political science courses can do for the potential wage earner is to supply him with a general background considered desirable by prospective employers in a wide range of fields.

It was once assumed that a political science major would take his B.A. degree to law school, graduate school, or into some kind of government work. These fields, of course, are still open. Political science is one of the majors considered useful by law schools. Such a major is usually considered necessary if the student elects to go on to graduate school in political science in preparation for college teaching. It can be useful in securing employment with any one of a number of relatively new governmental agencies such as the Office of Economic Opportunity. Similarly, it is an asset if the student hopes to enter training programs for such governmental departments as the Foreign Service.

A degree in political science now makes the student eligible for a great variety of positions in addition to the careers mentioned above. The range is infinite, and those who think they may be interested in exploring the possibilities would be well advised to seek the guidance of their college or department career counselor. For more immediate information, a brief sampling of the opportunities is given below.

One of the great economic phenomena since the end of World War II has been the expansion of American corporations to all corners of the globe. Although such foreign investment was not uncommon before 1945, the war's economic devastation of Europe opened that continent up to the capital of relatively unscathed American firms. More recently, the developing countries of Africa, Asia, and Latin America have been seeking private American capital. This means that there is a widespread need on the part of American corporations which have branches abroad or which deal with foreign governments for the services of people with some background in governmental affairs. Banks are but one example.

Within the United States, a different kind of economic expansion has taken place. The government's involvement in many different areas of life has been discussed above. Almost all such involvement implies the need for local, state, and federal governmental agencies to choose among a plethora of competing companies willing and able to contract for specific projects. The corporations, in turn, require personnel who have some idea of how the government goes about making decisions and how to deal with the government once a contract has been acquired. This is true of firms producing military uniforms, of those making advanced electronic equipment, of those contracting for highway projects, and of many others supplying goods or services. Private planning agencies and architectural firms, whether engaged in private work or in public urban programs, need liaison agents in dealing with the government. Their problems may range from relatively simple zoning requirements to the need for constant contact with the federal government during the planning of major urban renewal projects.

We have already pointed out that the major technique utilized by interest groups is that of lobbying. Some groups and individual corporations which lobby may not care to establish their own lobbying corps but may rely instead upon the expertise of private lobbying agencies. A background in government studies is invaluable to these agencies, which must have employees capable of threading their way both through the labyrinth of government bureaucracies and through the halls of the various legislatures. Similarly, voting analysis groups and public relations firms engaged in work for political parties and candidates require employees with some background in public opinion formation, voting studies, etc. This field should expand even further as politicians place more and more emphasis on the importance of polls in helping to select candidates and on the importance of public relations techniques in helping to get them elected.

One of the many effects of the growth of the mass media in the United States has resulted in bringing the aura of politics closer to the average man. Whether the media simply acquaint the average American with the superficial panoply of political life or actually aid him to a more sophisticated understanding of the political realities is an open question, but the fact remains that television and radio stations, newspapers, and news magazines find that they are devoting more and more of their time to political matters. Consequently, the various media are in need of personnel who possess some understanding of the political scene.

Once again, it should be emphasized that this is no more than a smattering of the possibilities. It should also be noted that a major in political science is neither direct nor, necessarily, sufficient training for any of the jobs discussed. What it can do is supply one of the most important qualifications, namely a generalized knowledge of the workings of the government and an acquaintance with the structure and dynamics of the political system. Courses in political science may also broaden the interest of students who have already decided upon or who will later decide upon careers outside political science proper. Potential architects or engineers may find a way to combine their primary interest with political science and go on to specialize in problems of urban renewal. Students looking forward to a career in journalism may decide to focus on the reporting of political affairs. An art student with a bent for cartoons may ultimately bring his interests together in a career as a political cartoonist.

Finally, it should be remembered that a major in political science may be of help in enabling a college graduate to obtain one of the many kinds of jobs open to all college graduates. Jobs in the civil service, in elementary and high school teaching, in advertising agencies, in the Peace Corps, in VISTA, etc., are all open to political science majors. It is truly no exaggeration to state that the possibilities are only as limited as your imagination.

CONCLUSION:
THE RELEVANCE OF
POLITICAL SCIENCE

In the preceding pages we have attempted to give you a glimpse into the world of political science by examining what political science is and what political scientists do. Political science is, of course, the study of government and their appurtenances (parties, groups, elections, etc.); more importantly, it is a part of the study of man and the world he has fashioned for himself. The proverbial Martian could learn a great deal about the strange creatures on earth by investigating no more than the political systems they have erected. If the record of the governments mankind has created is read carefully enough, it will yield an understanding of man's needs, his desires, his hopes, his ideals, his fears, his mistakes, and his triumphs.

The exciting thing about political science is that the record it analyzes is in a continuing state of renovation and renewal. Political scientists study the past: They explore the nature of governments that no longer exist; they pore over the early days of governments that are still with us. Their major interest, however, is the present and the future, and they study the past only for the currently applicable lessons it can teach. The events which concern political scientists are taking place today and will take place tomorrow and next week and next year. The generalizations discoverable in political history will be utilized by political scientists and politicians in the future. Political science does not deal primarily with dusty corners and old memories and long-forgotten events; its subject matter is as new as the role of television in electing candidates, or the legislative battles over the financing of the space program, or the attempts of newly created African nations to find and take their place in the world, or the impact of "black power" on urban politics.

The social sciences as a whole take as their subject matter the behavior of man in society: The values and customs and institutions and systems he utilizes in order to enhance his own life and to be able to exist alongside his fellowmen. Political science deals in particular with the values and customs and institutions and systems that comprise and surround the legal entity known as government. Government is the social creation which men endow with great authority and the right to use force because it is expected to respond when other institutions have proven incapable of solving the problems society insists must be solved.

James Madison believed that the existence of government proved that men were not angels; if they were angels, he felt, governments would not be necessary. Governments, in his eyes, were a reflection of man's inability to control his evil and grasping nature. A century later, Karl Marx postulated that when the communist millennium had been reached and men had learned the meaning of the good life, government would wither away as an unnecessary relic of a former age. Other theorists have viewed government more positively, seeing it as no more than a useful device by which men can join together to accomplish specific tasks. Whether or not government is a sign of the fallibility of humanity, there is no indication that it will disappear in the near future. Perhaps, as Aristotle wrote, man is a social animal, able to thrive only within the context of the kind of social organization made possible by government. Certainly, government has become more and more important and pervasive during the last century alone. It is routinely asked to handle a plethora of old problems and a continuously expanding host of new ones. It permeates all aspects of life in the highly industrialized societies, and it is currently being called upon to respond in novel and far-reaching ways to the problems of the emerging nations.

As government expands, so does political science. It not only has more material to absorb and analyze; it must also develop new techniques and methodologies if it is to remain as dynamic as its subject matter. American political science, which was once devoted primarily to American and Western European governments and theory, has as a matter of course come to include extensive research in the political affairs of Africa, Latin America, Asia, and Eastern Europe. Where it once held itself aloof from other disciplines, it has begun to incorporate the lessons of sociology, anthropology, and psychology, and to experiment with techniques devised by mathematicians and computer experts.

The effects of government action are all around you. Political science is an attempt to understand and explain and guide that action. It is a relevant and an exciting discipline. We hope you enjoy it.

FOR
ADDITIONAL READING

The following list represents only the smallest sample of books available in the various fields. It consists of a few classics and of a large body of general works, most of which can lead you to still further sources. Your instructor can undoubtedly also recommend titles for your particular area of study or interest.

THE NATURE OF POLITICAL SCIENCE

Charlesworth, James C. (ed.), *The Limits of Behavioralism in Political Science*. Philadelphia: American Academy of Political and Social Science, 1962.

Crick, Bernard, *The American Science of Politics*. Berkeley: University of California Press, 1959.

Dahl, Robert A., *Modern Political Analysis*. Englewood Cliffs, N.J.: Prentice-Hall, Inc., 1963.

Easton, David, *A Systems Analysis of Political Life*. New York: John Wiley & Sons, Inc., 1965.

—— (ed.), *Varieties of Political Theory*. Englewood Cliffs, N.J.: Prentice-Hall, Inc., 1966.

Hyneman, Charles, *The Study of Politics*. Urbana: University of Illinois Press, 1959.

Meehan, Eugene J., *The Theory and Method of Political Analysis*. Homewood, Ill.: Dorsey Press, 1965.

Pool, Ithiel, *et al.*, *Contemporary Political Science*. New York: McGraw-Hill Book Company, 1967.

Ranney, Austin (ed.), *Essays on the Behavioral Study of Politics*. Urbana: University of Illinois Press, 1962.

——, *The Governing of Men: An Introduction to Political Science*, rev. ed. New York: Holt, Rinehart & Winston, Inc., 1966.

Sorauf, Frank J., *Political Science: An Informal Overview*. Chicago: Merrill Company Publishers.

Van Dyke, Vernon, *Political Science: A Philosophical Analysis*. Stanford, Calif.: Stanford University Press, 1960.

AMERICAN GOVERNMENT

Bailey, Stephen K., *Congress Makes a Law*. New York: Columbia University Press, 1950.

Banfield, Edward C., and James Q. Wilson, *City Politics*. Cambridge: Harvard University Press and M.I.T. Press, 1963.

Beard, Charles A., *An Economic Interpretation of the Constitution of the United States*. New York: The Macmillan Company, 1913.

Binkley, Wilfred E., *President and Congress*. New York: Alfred A. Knopf, Inc., 1947.

Blau, Peter M., *Bureaucracy in Modern Society*. New York: Random House, Inc., 1956.

Bryce, James, *The American Commonwealth*. New York: The Macmillan Company, 1888.

Burns, James MacGregor, *The Deadlock of Democracy: Four Party Politics in America*. Englewood Cliffs, N.J.: Prentice-Hall, Inc., 1963.

Cardozo, Benjamin N., *The Nature of the Judicial Process*. New Haven, Conn.: Yale University Press, 1921.

Cater, Douglass, *Power in Washington*. New York: Random House, Inc., 1964.

Dahl, Robert A., *Who Governs? Democracy and Power in an American City*. New Haven, Conn.: Yale University Press, 1961.

De Tocqueville, Alexis, *Democracy in America*. New York: Oxford University Press, Inc., 1947, or any edition.

Freund, Paul A., *On Understanding the Supreme Court*. Boston: Little, Brown and Company, 1949.

Hofstadter, Richard, *The American Political Tradition*. New York: Alfred A. Knopf, Inc., 1951.

Key, V. O., Jr., *American State Politics: An Introduction*. New York: Alfred A. Knopf, Inc., 1956.

———, *Politics, Parties, and Pressure Groups*, 5th ed. New York: Crowell-Collier and Macmillan Incorporated, 1964.

———, *Southern Politics in State and Nation*. New York: Alfred A. Knopf, Inc., 1949.

Lazarsfeld, Paul, Bernard Berelson, and Hazel Gaudet, *The People's Choice*. New York: Columbia University Press, 1948.

Lewis, Anthony, *Gideon's Trumpet*. New York: Random House, Inc., 1964.

———, *et al., Portrait of a Decade: The Second American Revolution*. New York: Random House, Inc., 1964.

Lipset, Seymour M., *Political Man*. Garden City, N. Y.: Doubleday & Company, Inc., 1960.

McCloskey, Robert G., *The American Supreme Court*. Chicago: University of Chicago Press, 1960.

Mills, C. Wright, *The Power Elite*. New York: Oxford University Press, Inc., 1957.

Neustadt, Richard E., *Presidential Power*. New York: John Wiley & Sons, Inc., 1960.

Truman, David B., *The Governmental Process*. New York: Alfred A. Knopf, Inc., 1951.

White, Theodore H., *The Making of the President, 1960*. New York: Atheneum Publishers, 1961.

Wilson, Woodrow, *Congressional Government*. Boston: Houghton Mifflin Company, 1885.

COMPARATIVE GOVERNMENT

Almond, Gabriel A., and James S. Coleman, *The Politics of the Developing Areas.* Princeton, N. J.: Princeton University Press, 1960.

———, and Sidney Verba. *The Civic Culture.* Princeton, N.J.: Princeton University Press, 1963.

Arendt, Hannah, *Origins of Totalitarianism,* rev. ed. New York: Harcourt, Brace & World, Inc., 1966.

Bauer, Raymond A., Alexander Inkeles, and Clyde Kluckhohn, *How the Soviet System Works.* Cambridge: Harvard University Press, 1956.

Carter, Gwendolyn (ed.), *African One-Party States.* Ithaca, N.Y.: Cornell University Press, 1960.

Duverger, Maurice, *Political Parties.* New York: John Wiley & Sons, Inc., 1954.

Easton, Stewart C., *The Rise and Fall of Western Colonialism.* New York: Frederick A. Praeger, Inc., 1964.

Fainsod, Merle, *How Russia Is Ruled,* rev. ed. Cambridge: Harvard University Press, 1963.

Hyman, Herbert H., *Political Socialization.* New York: The Free Press, 1959.

Jennings, William I., *Cabinet Government,* 3rd ed. Cambridge, England: Cambridge University Press, 1959.

Johnson, John J., *Political Change in Latin America.* Stanford, Calif.: Stanford University Press, 1958.

Macridis, Roy C., *The Study of Comparative Government.* Garden City, N. Y., Doubleday & Company, Inc., 1955.

———, and Bernard E. Brown, *Comparative Politics: Notes and Readings,* rev. ed. Homewood, Ill.: Dorsey Press, 1964.

Mair, Lucy, *New Nations.* Chicago: University of Chicago Press, 1963.

Martz, John (ed.), *The Dynamics of Change in Latin American Politics.* Englewood Cliffs, N.J.: Prentice-Hall, Inc., 1965.

Neuman, Sigmund (ed.), *Modern Political Parties.* Chicago: University of Chicago Press, 1956.

Pye, Lucian W., *Aspects of Political Development.* Boston: Little, Brown and Company, 1966.

———, and Sidney Verba, *Political Culture and Political Development.* Princeton, N.J.: Princeton University Press, 1965.

Schapiro, Leonard, *The Communist Party of the Soviet Union.* New York: Random House, Inc., 1960.

Wallerstein, Immanuel, *Africa: The Politics of Independence.* New York: Vintage Books, 1961.

Ward, Robert E., and Roy C. Macridis (eds.), *Modern Political Systems: Asia.* Englewood Cliffs, N.J.: Prentice-Hall, Inc., 1963.

INTERNATIONAL RELATIONS

Almond, Gabriel A., *The American People and Foreign Policy*. New York: Harcourt, Brace & World, Inc., 1950.

Bailey, Thomas A., *The Art of Diplomacy*. New York: Appleton-Century-Crofts, 1968.

Bloomfield, Lincoln P., *The United Nations and United States Foreign Policy*, rev. ed. Boston: Little, Brown and Company, 1967.

Carr, Edward H., *The Twenty Years' Crisis, 1919–1939*, 2nd ed. New York: The Macmillan Company, 1962.

Claude, Inis, *Power and International Relations*. New York: Random House, Inc., 1963.

Halle, Louis J., *Men and Nations*. Princeton, N.J.: Princeton University Press, 1962.

Kaplan, Morton A., *System and Process in International Politics*. New York: John Wiley & Sons, Inc., 1957.

Kennan, George, *American Diplomacy 1900–1950*. Chicago: University of Chicago Press, 1951.

Larsen, Arthur, *When Nations Disagree*. Baton Rouge: Louisiana State University Press, 1961.

Morgenthau, Hans J., *Politics Among Nations*, 4th ed. New York: Alfred A. Knopf, Inc., 1967.

Organski, A. F. K., *World Politics*. New York: Alfred A. Knopf, Inc., 1958.

Padelford, Norman J., and George A. Lincoln, *The Dynamics of International Politics*. New York: The Macmillan Company, 1962.

Rosecrance, Richard N., *Action and Reaction in World Politics*. Boston: Little, Brown and Company, 1963.

Rosenau, James N. (ed.), *International Politics and Foreign Policy*. New York: The Free Press, 1961.

Scott, Andrew M., *The Functioning of the International Political System*. New York: The Macmillan Company, 1967.

Spanier, John, *American Foreign Policy Since World War II*, 3rd rev. ed. New York: Frederick A. Praeger, Inc., 1968.

———, *World Politics in an Age of Revolution*. New York: Frederick A. Praeger, Inc., 1967.

———, and Joseph L. Noger, *The Politics of Disarmament*. New York: Frederick A. Praeger, Inc., 1962.

Spiro, Herbert J., *Politics in Africa*. Englewood Cliffs, N.J.: Prentice-Hall, Inc., 1962.

Stoessinger, John G., *The Might of Nations*, rev. ed. New York: Random House, Inc., 1965.

Thompson, Kenneth W., *American Diplomacy and Emergent Patterns.* New York: New York University Press, 1962.

Ward, Barbara, *The Rich Nations and the Poor Nations.* New York: W. W. Norton & Company, Inc., 1962.

Wright, Quincy, *A Study of War,* abr. ed. Chicago: University of Chicago Press, 1965.

POLITICAL THEORY

Aristotle: *Politics* (any edition).

Barker, Ernest, *Political Thought of Plato and Aristotle.* New York: Russell & Russell, 1959.

Bluhm, William T., *Theories of the Political System: Classics of Political Thought and Modern Political Analysis.* Englewood Cliffs, N.J.: Prentice-Hall, Inc., 1965.

Brecht, Arnold, *Political Theory: The Foundations of Twentieth-Century Political Thought.* Princeton, N.J.: Princeton University Press, 1959.

Brinton, Crane, *Ideas and Men: The Story of Western Thought,* 2d ed. Englewood Cliffs, N.J.: Prentice-Hall, Inc., 1963.

Burns, Edward M., *Ideas in Conflict: The Political Theories of the Contemporary World.* New York: W. W. Norton & Company, Inc., 1960.

Cairns, Hungtington, *Legal Philosophy from Plato to Hegel.* Baltimore: The Johns Hopkins Press, 1949.

Ebenstein, William (ed.), *Great Political Thinkers,* 3rd ed. New York: Holt, Rinehart & Winston, Inc., 1960.

Hacker, Andrew, *Political Theory: Philosophy, Ideology, Science.* New York: The Macmillan Company, 1961.

Hobbes, Thomas, *Leviathan* (any edition).

Locke, John, *Civil Government* (any edition).

Machiavelli, Niccolo, *The Prince* (any edition).

McIlwain, Charles H., *The Growth of Political Thought in the West.* New York: The Macmillan Company, 1932.

Mill, John S., *On Liberty* (any edition).

Plato: *The Republic* (any edition).

Rousseau, Jean J., *Social Contract* (any edition).

Sabine, George H., *A History of Political Theory,* 3rd ed. New York: Holt, Rinehart & Winston, Inc., 1961.

Strauss, Leo, *Natural Right and History.* Chicago: University of Chicago Press, 1953.

———, and Joseph Cropsey, *History of Political Philosophy.* Skokie, Ill.: Rand McNally & Co., 1963.